GO
NO GO

GO
NO GO

IS YOUR BUSINESS IDEA READY TO LAUNCH?

LAURI HARRISON

TWENTY STEPS PRESS

Go. No Go. Is Your Business Idea Ready to Launch?

Published by Twenty Steps Press

Denver, CO

ISBN: 978-0-692-18923-8

BUSINESS / Entrepreneurship
BUSINESS / New Business Enterprises

Cover by Victoria Wolf
Interior design by Andrea Costantine

QUANTITY PURCHASES: Schools, companies, professional groups, clubs, and other organizations may qualify for special terms when ordering quantities of this title. For information, email lauri.harrison@gmail.com.

To Paul and Sam and extended family and close friends—
thank you for supporting me on this journey.

CONTENTS

Downloadable Templates from 20stepspublishing.com/
gonogo-templates/

- O **Checklist**: the handy marketing checklist to ensure you cover all aspects addressed in this book.

- O **Startup Action Plan Template**: an action plan template for your startup business.

- O **Launch Ideas Template:** launch ideas to consider if you are opening a physical store.

- O **Ophelia Dashboard Spreadsheet:** a sample spreadsheet template for Ophelia's metrics to monitor.

Share Your Business Story: earn an Amazon gift card. Details provided at the above URL.

INTRODUCTION

This book is written for budding entrepreneurs who need help determining if a business idea is worthwhile to launch as an actual business. My goal is to provide practical techniques to help you perform market research to validate the idea and then make a Go/No-Go decision to move forward with your business. You will not find gimmicks or quick-fix techniques here. I will show you how to create a solid foundation to start from that can set you up for success.

If you have an idea that you, and perhaps others, believe can solve a problem in the marketplace, and you do not have a marketing background, this book is for you. I will take you through a detailed process to confirm you have a valid product or service before you spend a penny on product development and marketing. For nearly two decades, I have consulted with start-ups and legacy businesses of all sizes. My favorite types of clients are start-ups because they are the most eager to learn and typically put the customer at the center of everything they do.

It would be ideal for me to work one-on-one with every start-up looking for someone they can trust. Since that's not a viable option, I decided to write this book as a guide to empower people to successfully research and validate their business idea before jumping into the creation of their actual business. It isn't rocket science, and you do not need a degree in marketing to win in business. What you *do* need is a solid understanding of the fundamentals for bringing a product or service to the marketplace. I will walk you through those fundamentals in a logical way, so you can apply what you're learning to your own business idea. You will learn how to identify the problems (pain points) you see in the marketplace that you would like to solve, and then you will determine if there is an audience willing to buy your product (the solution to the problem). This solid foundation sets you on a path for a successful launch and will help you build a loyal group of customers.

Here are some challenges a typical start-up might face:

○ Believing if you build it, they will come.

○ Just because you create a product or service to solve an existing problem doesn't always mean your product or service will be purchased. You need to confirm there is an audience (a market) for your solution, and you need confirmation the audience is *willing to pay* for the solution. Validating your business model is essential early in the process.

○ You just "know" there's a market for your product because friends and family have told you so.

○ Similarly, you may have invented the next best thing since sliced bread, but if no one is willing to pay for it, you won't have a viable business.

○ You believe your product will go viral from Day One.

○ Similar to "build it and they will come," creating awareness isn't as easy as you might think, despite the free social platforms at your disposal. You need to have your audience (your potential customers) believe in your purpose. Customers want to feel a connection to your brand and understand your company's reason for being before they consider what you have to offer. A value proposition is your solution to a problem for a specific target audience, which is unique when compared to other offerings in the marketplace. You will tailor the story about your value proposition specifically to your potential audience.

Throughout this book you will learn how to:

○ Address these basic questions:
  ○ What is the purpose of your business?
  ○ Which customers do you plan to serve?
  ○ What value would you like to create and deliver to those customers?
  ○ And many more.

○ Create a game plan to know where you are, where you want to go, and make a Go/No-Go decision to either move forward or refine your idea.

BONUS: Funding!

As a reader of this book, you will have an opportunity to submit your business idea for a chance to receive an Amazon $50 gift card. Details are at the end of the book.

WHY WOULD A BOOK LIKE THIS HELP YOU WITH YOUR BUSINESS IDEA?

Marketing, as a discipline, has dramatically changed in the past decade, not to mention in the past several years. Tried-and-true methods for success are no longer sufficient, and the basics are being rewritten. Companies who operate in the "business as usual" mode are not surviving. Remember when Blockbuster was the market leader in movie and game rentals? At its peak in 2004, Blockbuster had up to 60,000 employees and more than 9,000 stores. Just seven years later, in April 2011, Blockbuster assets were acquired by DISH Network during a bankruptcy auction. Just two years later, in 2013, DISH Network announced the closing of the last 300 company-owned Blockbuster stores. In less than a decade, disruptive technology had dramatically changed the customer experience and expectations for at-home entertainment.

The global economy dictates that it is important, now more than ever before, to monitor and leverage marketing trends, identify and pursue new opportunities, and be well poised to avoid threats. The competition has become more flexible, nimble, and global. Therefore, sustainable businesses have to become proactive, rather than reactive, to what's happening in the marketplace, in order to take control of their destinies. In the past few years, social media marketing has become a strategic imperative. Businesses of any size can build an army of brand advocates, and this allows them to obtain direct feedback and respond to customers in real-time. *This is one-to-one marketing at its finest.* This interactive, two-way dialogue is the new normal for customer engagement and experience. Companies such as Zappos and Airbnb are performing quite well, earning $1 billion in revenues in less than a decade after launching their respective businesses. They have written a new rule book for how to do it right. Social media marketing is just one reason why marketing is no longer limited to a department within a company. As marketing guru Seth Godin says, "Everyone is a marketer." This is critical to success in today's world. Every employee within an organization has become an extension of the marketing department, as has every customer, partner, and supplier for your business.

The ultimate goals for a business are to:

○ Have a specific and clear purpose or reason for being (ideally making an impact in some way).

○ Create and deliver value to your customers.

○ Build long-term, profitable customer relationships.

○ Nurture employee and customer experiences.

○ Receive valuable customer insights and incorporate them back into the value delivered.

The process of getting a product or service to market is not as easy as it used to be. Plenty of obstacles must be overcome to build awareness and trust, plus to showcase value. Today, businesses are implementing a variety of online and offline marketing initiatives to overcome these obstacles and to focus on building social communities, also known as "tribes," in order to gain a competitive advantage and build a solid customer base. Businesses must pay attention to the constant changes that are all around them. It's easy to track and monitor what your competitors are up to on the social web. This book will cover the concepts that are fundamental to marketing and marketing management for your start-up. By understanding these concepts, you can create a marketing strategy to position your organization for success.

You can apply what you learn in a couple of ways. First, consider how each step relates to your business or business idea as you read through each section. Second, read the entire book, see how the best practices are applied to the fictitious business example, and then apply best practices to your business.

Also, as you review this book, you may come across unfamiliar terminology. It may be useful to review the glossary at the end of this book prior to getting started.

The book takes you through the process of making a decision about your business idea with your eyes wide open. The time you spend upfront working on this process will ultimately save you time, money, and human resources.

During this process, you will conduct research, use the research findings to define and plan what your business ultimately sets out to do, and evaluate the information you gathered and synthesized. I will provide tools to help organize your information, so you will be well armed to make a rational Go/No-Go decision.

Let's get started. We have a lot of ground to cover vetting your business idea, so you don't bet the farm on an offering no one is willing to buy. Are you ready? Let's discover what you really need to know to confidently move from business idea to business launch and success.

CHAPTER 1

YOU HAVE A NEW BUSINESS IDEA. NOW WHAT?

"I have a great product idea, and I'm ready to launch my business right now!"

"Everyone tells me that my product idea will sell like hotcakes."

"This is definitely a million-dollar idea."

"I need to go on *Shark Tank* because they will love it."

Do any of those quotes sound familiar to you? I have been listening to these types of statements for nearly twenty years. I'm a product and marketing consultant and also teach a graduate-level course on product and marketing strategy. I have spoken with hundreds of people who want to fulfill the American Dream and start their own business. It seems "easy to get started," and many take the leap into entrepreneurship before they are ready.

The allure of being your own boss, making your own hours,

and having work/life balance is the primary driver for many to start their own business. For others, they want to take their passion, project, or hobby to the next level. Unfortunately, statistics don't lie. According to the US Small Business Administration, over 50% of small businesses fail in the first year and 95% fail within the first five years. The primary reason for small businesses failure is **cash flow** problems. If no one is willing to buy your solution, cash is not coming through the door.

Cash flow can be better managed if you use the right tools and execute best practices to get your business off the ground. We will start with the basics. I will provide a voice of reason to show you where and how to begin. If this sounds intriguing to you, read on.

This section will guide you through best practice approaches to create and deliver value. It's similar to building a solid foundation for your house. Once the foundation has been created, you can build whatever you would like from there.

You are about to take an honest look at your new business idea. By investing in the foundation now, you will save time and money down the road on wasted efforts or get-rich-quick schemes. Once you complete this activity, you will know where you are, which I refer to as Point A: the classic "You are here!" on a map.

Here's a checklist of what will be covered in this section:

O Do your homework. **Market research**: understanding the competition and the market and why it is an important process.

O Define the **"why"**: your company's reason for being;

the impact your company has on the world.

○ Define the **"what"**: this is your value proposition, the benefits provided by your solution. It addresses how you compare to your competition.

○ Define the **"who"**: your target customers; they must be reachable and measurable.

○ Create your **point of view (POV)**: truly understand the needs of your customer.

○ Create your **Product Vision Statement.**

○ **Test your product offering** on a select group of customers; refine it as needed, based on feedback.

○ Define the **"how much"**: create a pricing strategy.

○ Define the **"where"**: how your target customer will buy your product.

○ Define **how to promote**: how your target customers will learn about your value proposition.

○ Conduct **a SWOT analysis**: analyze the strengths, weaknesses, opportunities, and threats of and to your business: a truthful reality check.

WHY START HERE?

Throughout my consulting career, I have worked with companies of all sizes on projects large and small. I noted a similar theme across them all—a lack of information about the true reality. It didn't matter if I was helping with product strategy, marketing strategy, or sales strategy. A common weakness was a lack of understanding about the **problems** they were solving with their solutions (products and services) and **for whom** they were solving those problems. Not only that, there was a fundamental lack of understanding about how their solutions were truly **unique** in the marketplace. In addition, the organization's **reason for being** was not fully understood internally by employees or externally by their potential audience.

Without this basic understanding, there will not be a solid foundation to launch and grow your business.

You need to address the fundamentals, what I refer to as the "upstream work." If you focus your time, energy, and resources on the upstream work, the downstream process of executing marketing and sales strategies will be a lot easier. Do the heavy lifting early on, so you know you have something that does have **value** for **particular types of customers** who have also expressed a **willingness to *buy* it**. Nail that, and you have established a strong foundation from the start.

Let me provide some examples:

Twitter created an amazing social platform. It leveled the communications playing field for corporate brands and individual citizen brands. Everyone's voice can be heard. Everyone can have real-time access to their favorite topics, people of interest, and other things they care about, as a business or as an individual. The value is enormous and the price remains *free!*

Twitter was counting on building a user base that would soar to the same heights as Facebook and other leading social networks. According to Statista.com, as of the first quarter of 2017, Twitter had 328 million monthly active users. Those numbers pale in comparison to Facebook, which self-reports 1.8 billion monthly active users as of December 2016 (2). Although Twitter was founded in 2006, a profitable business model still eludes them.

Let's take a look at Twitter's upstream activities:

○ **Did they solve a problem in the marketplace?** Yes. They became the first platform to provide real-time information to anyone around the globe, originally with a 140-character limit. As of November 2017, Twitter doubled the character count to 280.

○ **Did they target specific types of customers?** No. They opened it up to "the world"—for anyone to use, including businesses.

○ **Did they confirm customer willingness to buy the product?** No. They provided it free to all users, both individuals and organizations. Twitter's primary revenue stream is based on advertising revenue: individuals and businesses pay a fee to promote tweets and accounts. The second revenue stream is from selling data from tweets and user profiles (Unicornomy, 2017.) How has their business model turned out? As of early 2017, they are still struggling to become profitable (Gottfried, 2017.)

Twitter had a record high valuation of $40 billion in 2013; as of May 2017, the valuation was hovering near $13 billion. Why such a dramatic drop within a short timeframe? The company has yet to turn a profit.

Let's shift gears and discuss a trendy smartphone accessory called PopSockets, available at popsockets.com. A college professor, David Barnett, was frustrated by his earbuds getting constantly tangled. Every time he wanted to use them, he had to struggle to straighten them out before he could put them in his ears. This led to an idea to create an attachment for the back of his smartphone case to keep the cords tangle-free. He tried some rudimentary concepts, such as sticking a big button to the back of his phone, but eventually designed what is in the market today: a removable, round object that adheres to your phone or case.

Visit popsockets.com to learn more about the product and explore their companion products.

The PopSocket can pop out, via the collapsible accordion so you can wrap your earbud cords around it, then pop the accordion back down to your phone to make it less bulky. At least, that's what the founder thought it would be used for.

After a successful Kickstarter campaign and over one million products sold, the true utility of the product came from teens and college students using it as a handgrip to hold their phone while they took a selfie (a self-portrait), as well as a kickstand to prop up their phone while watching videos or having a video chat.

The value proposition evolved from a wrap for earbud cords to a grip and a kickstand. This is now the trifecta in smartphone accessories. Word-of-mouth has caused this product to go viral, and organizations buy the product in large quantities with their logo printed on them to hand out at conferences. Suddenly, the target customers grew from just consumers to the business market. The rest is history for the company. They have patented their product design and are expanding their product portfolio to include other companion products. **Sometimes the solution you create to solve a specific problem ends up being used for completely different purposes by your customers.**

Let's review the fundamentals for the PopSocket product idea and the upstream activities:

○ **Did they solve a problem in the marketplace?** Yes. Initially the problem was simply to keep earbud cords tangle-free.

○ **Did they target specific types of customers?** Yes. People with smartphones who use earbuds.

○ **Did they confirm customer willingness to buy the product?** Yes. Through a Kickstarter campaign, 520 backers pledged $18,591 to help bring their project to life (Kickstarter, 2018.) The product was refined, as customers gave feedback as to how they were using the product and the types of customizations they wanted for designs, colors, and imagery. After all, a smartphone isn't just a device; for many, it's a means of self-expression. Therefore the case, headphones (or earbuds) and accessories (such as a PopSocket) need to match customer preferences for self-expression.

It's no wonder PopSockets continue to thrive and grow as they evolve the product value, based on input from their consumer and business audiences.

The same rules apply to *your* business idea. It's time to get out there, see what your competitors are doing and what trends are occurring in the marketplace, and identify your company's reason for being as a player in the marketplace.

CHAPTER 2

DO YOUR HOMEWORK: IS YOUR IDEA ALREADY OUT THERE

I can't emphasize this market research step enough. It's one of the most critical parts of building a solid foundation for a business. Yet, many companies often skip this step because they believe their idea is *Shark Tank*-worthy (6) and it will sell itself. I strongly caution you to avoid skipping the market research step before you move full steam ahead with your business idea. Ego and arrogance can provide a lot of confidence and passion to "just go for it." However, the harsh realities of what is happening in the marketplace may crush you if you don't take time for the discovery process.

The first place to start is with Google or your favorite search engine. Start typing in keywords related to your business idea, and look at the search results. Scan the results to identify similar types of products or solutions. Start making a list of those competitors. You don't need a comprehensive list of hundreds of companies. Simply start with a reasonable number, such as five to ten, or whatever number you feel comfortable with. Then perform a deep dive into those companies to see what their value proposition is and their reason for being. It is also advisable to search for similar substitute products and services, also known as "indirect competitors." The more you know about direct and indirect competition and alternative solutions, the better off you will be as you create your company's reason for being and value proposition. You will know what you need to do to stand out and provide more impact.

One of my favorite ways to capture competitive analysis data is to create a table in Microsoft Word or use tabs in Microsoft Excel to organize the data I collect. Here are the primary elements you should be collecting:

- Company name
- Headquarters location
- Year the company was founded
- Number of employees
- Corporate tagline
- Website URL
- Social media presence: Facebook, Twitter, SnapChat, Instagram, Pinterest
- Any others you may want to track
- Key stats

Collect newsworthy information.

An easy way to get information about company revenues, partnerships, key customers, new products, and more is from the company website in their Pressroom, Newsroom, or Investor Relations section.

If the company website doesn't have any of the above, look for press releases and company news on the web. Companies love to boast about their milestones and accomplishments, their participation at industry conferences, and so much more. You can find the press releases on their website or in search engine results. Capture the significant newsworthy data. It may help discover areas you hadn't thought about or types of customers to pursue.

Summarize Their Reason for Being

Many organizations state their core values, mission, and vision in the About Us page of their website. This information answers the question about why they are in business—their "reason for being."

If they are a publicly held company, you can review their SEC filings (US Securities and Exchange Commission) at sec.gov for in-depth insight.

Products Provided

You don't have to list every product they sell, just the products most similar to your offering.

Capture What's Unique About Their Products: Their Unique Selling Proposition (USP)

Capture what they say regarding the uniqueness of their

offering. Often times, you may discover it's not really unique. If other companies can say the exact same thing about their product or service, then it is not unique. The USP will help you narrow your own "differentiators," which are the aspects of the product that separate you from the competition. This correlates directly to your value proposition.

Be Mindful of Feature-by-Feature Analysis, as Compared to Your Product

This is a losing game and suggests your solution is a commodity: the "widgets" you produce and sell are about the same as your competitor's. However, if your value is superior, price doesn't matter. Price comparisons are not a way to build a business for the long haul. The real value your business provides goes above and beyond the price points of the widgets you sell. The value is also the greater purpose of your company, your story about why the business exists, and what you set out to do for the world. Your business will likely attract loyal customers who are advocates for your business, and the revenues will pour in. There should be meaning and a sense of purpose for your business before you make your first sale.

KEY TAKEAWAYS

This is where you write the "so what" or key insights about this competitor. It could be their biggest strength, which poses as a challenge for you to conquer. It could be the opportunity the company has because they just closed a round of funding with investors. Whatever it is, these are your "aha!" discoveries about this competitor.

When you have a decent list of five to ten competitors with the above-mentioned data collected, set up alerts to monitor their actions moving forward. You will also be "in the know" about your competitor's activities.

MONITOR YOUR COMPETITORS

The best way to monitor your top competitors is to follow them on social media, sign up as an email subscriber to their newsletter, and create Google Alerts. Google Alerts (google.com/alerts) allow you to track certain keywords, such as company names or product names, so when a press release, article, or blog is posted, you will receive the alert in your inbox. You can turn alerts on or off, and you can edit them to refine the search, so your inbox doesn't blow up with a lot of unrelated information.

In addition, platforms such as Google News (news.google.com) and Flipboard (flipboard.com) are great tools to read and track on a daily basis the areas of interest to you, without having to fill your inbox with hundreds of alerts. You can personalize your news page to show any news topic. This creates an e-newspaper catered to all the areas you are interested in. Select your favorite news resource to help you easily stay up-to-date with competitor activities.

Why is this important? As I mentioned earlier, **everyone is a marketer, as well as a consumer.** Those who stay informed and also proactively participate in social media, write blog posts, and engage with their tribe (their like-minded followers), will stay ahead of the competition and build a thriving community of supporters for their products.

MARKET RESEARCH FOR A BUSINESS IDEA

I have created a fictitious person and business idea as an example to use throughout this book. I hope the continuity of this fictional business will bring context to the process for you.

Here is the back story:

Ophelia has a passion for making delicious chocolate. She has been making small batches of chocolates as gifts to share with friends and family for years. Everyone begs Ophelia to share her secret recipe, but she always declines. Ophelia has perfected a special family recipe, which has been passed down for generations. The recipe includes secret ingredients and techniques to make delicious chocolates that are healthy by today's standards, as the chocolate is lactose-free and sugar-free. Ophelia would like to transform her hobby into a business.

Ophelia hopes her popularity with friends and family can spill over to the community at large. For years, she thought about renting a commercial kitchen and hiring helpers to create larger batches to sell to a broader audience. Recently, she discovered there was an opportunity to rent the perfect storefront location in the town center, where an old-fashioned candy shop used to be. It had been family run since the early 1900s and recently closed its doors. It's an ideal scenario for Ophelia, as the location has a commercial kitchen in the back. Ophelia's dream is to make her healthy chocolates available to a larger audience. But before making a firm commitment, Ophelia wants to be sure she is properly set up for success.

Ophelia and her friends and family have noted there aren't many choices available for chocolates without lactose and raw sugar ingredients. After visiting organic sections of grocery stores and stores catering to health-conscious customers, Ophelia found plenty of chocolate products on the shelves. However, she couldn't find any products similar to her own. Even the chocolates with the highest cocoa percentage included raw sugar or some form of milk product. Ophelia purchased the products and realized the taste was very bitter and the products were rather expensive.

Ophelia expanded her research online, trying to find chocolate products without lactose and sugar. She was stunned to discover there were plenty of sugar substitutes included in most of the chocolate products, but just about every brand contained milk products. Ophelia realized she was on to something truly unique. Not only did her chocolates eliminate sugar and sugar substitutes but also milk products; the taste was undeniably delicious. Ophelia's friends and family described the chocolates as decadent and mouthwatering. The winning elements were the scrumptious, delicious taste, as well as the health benefits of being lactose and sugar-free.

Throughout this book, I will use the header "Let's Put It Into Action" to apply key elements to this fictitious business idea.

Now that I've introduced Ophelia and her business idea, let's get back to the basics.

CHAPTER 3

DEFINE THE PROBLEM: WHAT, WHO, AND WHY

Today, it's easy to launch a business, and there is no shortage of great business ideas. Most new entrepreneurs believe market conditions are right, the product is right, and the timing is right. Yet, there are plenty of "if only" reasons why small businesses fail.

If only:

- The funding came through.
- The right business partner came along.
- The right big contract came in.
- Etc.

If you watch the TV show *Shark Tank*, you will see the passion, energy, and ambition of the entrepreneurs looking for at least one of the sharks to invest in their business. Even the seemingly great ideas don't attract a shark investor for any number of reasons:

O They do not believe in the entrepreneur's purpose for creating the business.

O They do not understand the problem being solved.

O It is unclear that there is potential reach within an addressable market or if there really is a market to target.

O There is uncertainty about the ability to scale sales.

O It is unclear how quickly they can recoup their investment, plus earn a tidy profit.

Start-ups need more than a hook to build a sustainable and profitable business. **They need a solid value proposition and reachable target audience willing to pay for the value**.

Let's start with a few fundamental questions you need to answer to know if your business idea has the potential for success. (For simplicity, throughout the book I will use the term "product" to mean either a product or a service.)

What is the problem you are trying to solve with your product? Hint: Pick just one or two problems to solve; do not create a laundry list. You need to be very focused. Tackling too many problems at one time makes it difficult to do the one thing right. You can address the other problems later on.

Who are you trying to solve the problem for?

○ Do you *really* understand the needs of customers you want to sell to?

○ How does your product solve their problems or pain points?

○ Who are they? Can you articulate who they are? Are they reachable and measurable? Can you define them by gender, age, lifestyle, or other characteristics such as "moms twenty-five to forty" or "parents of five to twelve-year-olds" or "single men who live and work in urban areas"?

You need to be as specific as possible. This is just as important as understanding the problem you are trying to solve with your product. If you don't really know who potential customers are, it will be difficult to reach them with your message. There can be multiple target audiences representing various market segments. You should prioritize the core market segment you would like to reach. The other market segments can have a lower priority. This prioritization allows you to maximize your promotions and outreach much more effectively.

Once you know who your target audiences are, you can tailor your messaging, so it is meaningful to them and addresses their specific pain points. You will need to discover where your target audiences look for information when they need to solve a problem and which influencers they listen to for recommendations. These efforts will provide a bulls-eye approach to your value creation and delivery, as well as messaging formats. You will know who your customers are, where they live, and where they get their information. A one-size-fits-all approach to messaging could work, which is called mass marketing. However, mass marketing is akin to throwing spaghetti on the wall to see what sticks. It can be an incredible waste of time, money, and other resources.

Why does this problem need to be solved for this type of customer?

O Does your business exist solely to solve this problem? What is the reason or purpose of the business? The company's reason for being is the reason your customers will buy from you. This is where loyalty comes into play. People buy from brands they feel connected to. Companies such as TOMS Shoes have a "buy one, give one" model. TOMS gives away a pair of shoes for every pair purchased. Customers can also sign up to help deliver the shoes to those in need. TOMS Shoes customers are loyal because their purchase has a purpose, and they want to be part of that bigger purpose.

O Other than earn profits, what does the business aim to do? What are the core values of the business: basically, what does your business stand for (what is your mission)? What makes your product or business idea unique? Do you understand why customers will select your product over others?

O What is your "brand promise"? The brand promise is what the company promises to provide those who interact with their brand. The promise helps solidify the relationship you have with your customers. Ideally, a strong brand will evoke emotion and inspire people to connect to your brand. Apple, Inc. is a brand that evokes a very strong emotional response from loyal customers. Their brand promise is to "think differently." Apple doesn't accept the status quo and creates products that provide an exceptional experience. The company wants customers to expect more than the status quo as well.

The above questions are important to address in order to gain a firm understanding of why the business exists, the problem you are solving, and for whom you are solving it. Once this foundational level is articulated, you will have the information you need to proceed with product development, as well as messaging to be used later on when you launch your business.

LET'S PUT IT INTO ACTION

Now we will take a look at how Ophelia will define the "what," "who," and "why" for the problem she is trying to solve for her customers.

Define "What"

Problem: it is difficult to find delicious chocolates without lactose or sugar ingredients.

Solution: Ophelia creates chocolates using all natural ingredients that provide healthful benefits; her chocolates are sugar-free and lactose-free, yet taste delicious, not bitter. "Delicious chocolates without lactose or sugar ingredients."

Define "Who"

Identify the potential audience looking for a solution to the problem: health-conscious consumers who desire delicious chocolate treats, without lactose or sugar added. In addition, diabetics and lactose-intolerant groups are ideal to target, since 65 percent of the human population has a reduced ability to digest lactose after infancy (The Physicians Committee, 2011.) and nearly 10 percent have diabetes (CDC, 2018.)

"Why" Create This Business and These Chocolates?

This is very apparent for Ophelia: She wants to help people with special dietary needs by providing decadent and delicious treats they typically cannot have. However, she doesn't need to limit her customer base to those with special dietary needs—anyone can benefit from the healthy ingredients.

Does Ophelia Understand the Needs of Potential Customers and How Her Chocolates Solve Their Problem?

Yes. She understands it is frustrating to find chocolate without lactose and sugar ingredients at physical stores or online.

Can Ophelia articulate who the potential customers are?

Yes: health-conscious eaters of chocolate who must eliminate or limit dairy and sugar in their diets. People with lactose intolerance and diabetes are primary target customers. Secondary customers are anyone who loves delicious chocolate and would appreciate the health benefits of her product.

Ophelia sees the need in the marketplace, has a solution based on her family's secret recipe, and also identified the initial target customer groups. She is ready to further the discovery process and continue deciding to Go/No-Go on launching her business idea: Ophelia's Chocolates.

CREATE YOUR POINT OF VIEW (POV)

A point of view (POV) is a clearly articulated problem statement. It becomes the North Star or guidepost to ensure you are solving the **right problem** for the **right audience** for the **right reason**.

The POV aligns your focus as you build and test your idea with potential customers and incorporate their feedback before you go to market. **The process of seeking to understand your customer puts you in *their* shoes. It's the only way to fully gain empathy for your potential customers.** Once you have deep empathy around pain points, you want to ensure you have a laser focus as you refine your product.

The POV is comprised of three parts: user, need, and insight. Think about using index cards as a tool to succinctly capture your insights and understanding about the user of your product (customer).

The structure looks like this:

A User Needs to "Do *or* Feel Something" (Action) Because of the Insight you Obtained While Seeking to Understand Their Problem

Here's how you can break it down:

User: a detailed description of your customer.

Action: the steps the user must take to address their pain points (or problems).

Insight: your discovery of why the problem is important or significant to potential customers and your understanding of the risk of ignoring the problem.

LET'S PUT IT INTO ACTION

Ophelia's Chocolates has the following POV:

User: people with health conditions, such as lactose intolerance and diabetes.

Action: pursue special diets that require lactose-free and sugar-free ingredients.

Insight: lactose and sugar-based ingredients can be life-threatening to some individuals.

Ophelia crafts her POV into the following summary:

"People with health conditions such as lactose intolerance and diabetes have special diets that require lactose-free and sugar-free ingredients because eating sugar or lactose can be life-threatening to them."

Now, when Ophelia creates new chocolate products, she can come back to her POV to ensure she is staying focused on her core mission for creating lactose-free and sugar-free chocolates. The fact that Ophelia's chocolates are rich-tasting and delicious is a bonus!

CREATE YOUR PRODUCT VISION STATEMENT

A product vision statement represents the essence of a product and describes the value proposition you intend to deliver. The statement has six parts:

For (*target customer*)
Who (*statement of need or opportunity*)
The (*product name*) is a (*product category*)
That (*key benefit reason to buy*)
Unlike (*primary competitive alternatives*)
Our product (*statement of primary differentiation*)

How does this product vision statement resonate with you and the elevator pitch you use to describe your products? The statement should be accurate and provide a sense of the value you plan to create and deliver.

Can you say the vision statement in less than thirty seconds? If not, refine it until you can.

LET'S PUT IT INTO ACTION

Ophelia's Chocolates has the following product vision statement:

For people with special dietary needs
Who indulge in sweets
Ophelia's Chocolates are a healthy chocolate treat
That is lactose-free and sugar-free and delicious
Unlike similar products on the market that have a bland or bitter taste
Our product tastes decadent and indulgent, without the harmful health effects.

Summary

"For people with special dietary needs who indulge in sweets, Ophelia's Chocolates are a healthy chocolate treat that are lactose-free and sugar-free. Unlike similar products on the market that have a bland or bitter taste, our chocolate tastes decadent and indulgent, without the harmful health effects."

Ophelia has applied her deep understanding of specific health conditions to create chocolate that satisfies cravings for sweets, does not have harmful ingredients, and tastes delicious, particularly in comparison to alternative healthy chocolate products.

CHAPTER 4

TEST YOUR IDEA

Before you go too far creating your product, you want to mitigate risk and **ensure you are building the right value to solve a specific problem for a specific group of customers who are willing to pay for your solution**. Show potential target customers the product, obtain feedback, and incorporate insights into your solution. This is your opportunity to ask how much they would be willing to pay for the product or service and run potential pricing by them. The discussions can be very enlightening. You may learn your price is too high or too low, or they wouldn't pay anything at all because they have a substitute they would rather use. Take all the observations and insights to heart and do some soul-searching, especially if major red flags come up that you did not expect.

This would be a good time to make necessary adjustments to the value proposition and potential price. Perhaps you need to do some number crunching to see if the adjustments are worthwhile for you to pursue. You get to make the final decision regarding the level of risk you are willing to take versus the potential reward you could receive once you go to market. Now is the time for a Go/No-Go decision, or Potentially Go (with caution and with adjustments).

LET'S PUT IT INTO ACTION

Ophelia has been collecting feedback from potential customers for quite some time. In addition to giving chocolates as gifts to friends and family, she offered free samples at local farmer's markets and sold small batches of chocolates.

Ophelia's taste tests amongst family, friends, and members of the community have shown the chocolates are very desirable. In general, there has been disbelief that something that tastes so good can actually provide health benefits. Ophelia has added to her original messaging that her chocolates are lactose-free and sugar-free; she now also states that they include antioxidants, which are beneficial to the heart. Ophelia has validated and enhanced the value proposition she is providing to customers. As far as pricing, Ophelia's friends and family have paid her for her products when she made special orders and gift baskets. But she realizes her personal community does not have price sensitivity because they are trying to support her. It would be wise for Ophelia to talk to people during taste tests who are not in her community, meaning not friends and family, to obtain more objective feedback on pricing.

Once Ophelia is armed with that information, she has every piece of product data she needs to make a Go/No-Go decision about transforming her hobby into a real business. She also has been recording what people have said about her chocolates during taste tests. This will be helpful information for her marketing freelancer, who will incorporate the feedback into the overall company messaging. Tailored messaging to each target audience is paramount to success.

CHAPTER 5

MARKETING DECISIONS:
PRICE, PLACE, AND PROMOTION

The second area to focus on is defining the pricing strategy for your product. A solid pricing strategy is easier said than done. As a business owner, you may want to recoup your investment as quickly as possible; therefore, you may select higher prices to increase profit margins from Day One. Or perhaps you want to quickly gain traction in the marketplace and sell as many products as possible. Therefore, the focus is on quantity sold: price lower to sell higher volume early on. Or you simply want to ensure you break even or make a slight profit initially, so you price based on your costs, with a slight margin.

Whatever makes sense for you and your business is how you should tackle the pricing strategy. A good rule of thumb is to keep it simple! Although this book does not cover financial analyses, you should work with a bookkeeper or accountant to help you understand your total costs and help you with projections for expenses and sales. It will save you the headache later on. It's best to have a professional begin early on as you establish your business, so you understand the implications of business insurance, liability insurance, sales tax, and other areas pertinent to your specific business. You don't need to hire an expensive accounting firm. Look for a boutique accounting shop or freelancer in your area and ask for recommendations from other small business owners. The local Chamber of Commerce will have a directory of service providers, as well as leads groups to join. That may be your best bet as a place to start, unless of course you're a QuickBooks pro and prefer to do it all yourself. That's fine too.

Be sure to run "what if" scenarios for various prices and units sold, so you can comfortably set your price and know what you need for sales on a daily, weekly, monthly, quarterly, and annual basis.

Areas to consider:

O Is your price set based on cost-plus profit margin? Or is it set based on value? For example, if you make necklaces by hand, the materials may cost you $10, but you spend time making it. To cover your time, you add 200% margin to ensure you make a profit, which is a $20 margin. Now you price the necklace at $30; this is pricing based on cost-plus profit. On the other hand, perhaps the value of that product is worth much more than $30 because you make a limited number of necklaces and they are highly desired by your target customers. Due to the limited supply available, you price the necklace $100. This is value pricing.

O Do you know if your customers are sensitive to price and price increases? Have you asked your target customers how much they are willing to spend on your product? *If no one is willing to pay, it's not worth building it in the first place.*

It is challenging for me when I receive requests from entrepreneurs to help them essentially throw a Hail Mary pass to hit their numbers at the end of a quarter or fiscal year. It's as if they hope a magic formula exists: that if X dollars are spent on marketing activities, then it will reap revenues of $XXX. In some industries, that might be the case, but it's not the norm. Unfortunately, if you created an amazing product that solves a real problem, but your target customer is not compelled enough to buy your product, you're out of luck. This is the reason you need to understand who your potential customers are, why they need your product to solve their problem, and if they are willing to buy it.

Once you decide on a price for the product, then it's time to figure out where your potential customers can buy it.

LET'S PUT IT INTO ACTION

Ophelia has a compelling product to help people with special dietary needs, but she can also cater to health-conscious eaters who would like a delicious chocolate treat without the guilt or the harmful ingredients. Ophelia's friends and family gush over her gift boxes and product displays at farmer's markets and special events. She has created the chocolates for her own love of chocolate, but also for her passion in helping others feel good. Previously, pricing was never a consideration, since she sold chocolates for a flat rate at the farmer's market. Ophelia had no idea what her total costs were for ingredients and packaging, not to mention the time spent creating the batches and the value of her family's secret recipe. She decided to put together her receipts for the current year and put them into a spreadsheet, just as a place to start and to prevent her from making mathematical errors from doing it by hand.

Ophelia discovered that her expenses were quite a bit higher than she had thought they would be. She sold her chocolate in three ways: by the piece, box, and bar. She knew she had to build up a pricing scheme to accommodate how many pieces and bars she could get out of a batch, what the total cost of the ingredients were per batch, and what the price point would be to break even for a batch. This number would allow her to price by piece, box, and bar.

For our purposes, let's say the total cost of ingredients is $125 per batch and one batch produces 500 pieces.

$125 cost / 500 = $0.25 per piece to break even, based only on hard costs, such as raw materials.

When she makes a batch for bars, it's the same cost per batch and one batch produces 50 bars.

$125 cost/50 = $2.50 per bar to break even.

This is a good starting point for Ophelia. She can add in a margin to recoup some of the start-up costs to form her business, and it's a price people would still be willing to pay, based on her experience selling at farmer's markets.

Cost = $0.25 per piece.　　Retail price = $0.50
Cost = $2.50 per bar.　　Retail price = $5.00

Ophelia knows she is in the ballpark of other healthy chocolate bars that are available in stores and are approximately the same size.

Now Ophelia can bundle pieces into boxes and come up with pricing for four pieces, eight pieces, and twelve pieces.

Although this book does not cover business plans, it is important to have full insight into all costs and sales projections in order to understand the amount of risk you are going to take before you officially go into business. Pricing for Ophelia's Chocolates is purposely designed to be simplistic in nature. The above example doesn't consider the machinery Ophelia uses and costs associated for electricity and water. The pricing does not incorporate the cost of packaging. Ophelia's packaging consists of boxes made of recycled materials, branded labels on the box top, and a ribbon. Bars are simply in a paper wrapper with a label she creates on her own computer. Ideally, at some point in the future, Ophelia would add in the costs for packaging, labels, and ribbons into the price of the product.

WHERE WILL CUSTOMERS BUY YOUR PRODUCT?

Perhaps you have a physical storefront, as well as an e-commerce storefront. This is known as a "click and brick" business. If you can handle the logistics of shipping online orders (via a website, social platform, mobile app, etc.), it's a terrific way to build a global audience. Nowadays, it's easier than ever to have a professional presence and attract new buyers. What used to cost small businesses tens of thousands of dollars for a website can be done for less than $100/month, or even for free. I will cover more specifics on this topic later in the book. In the meantime, you should consider a "mobile first" strategy to get your product sold online. That means create your own sales channels, partner with other channels, and/or allow others to resell your products online first.

A wonderful example of leveraging click and brick is Domino's Pizza. They have their sales channels down to a science and allow you to order via Anyware, a very clever and innovative strategy for their business. Once you create an online account, you enter the default "easy order" into your account, so you can instantly order the same thing from many different mediums. Domino's provides its customers with the ability to phone in an order, text an order, tweet an order, use an app to order, use Amazon Echo to place an order verbally, order on a SmartTV via app, place an order from your car (if you have Ford with SYNC Applink), order from a smartwatch, and last—but not least—order from your computer. Domino's has made it extremely easy for their customers to order pizza.

Once you are open for business, you need an organized way to track your sales and to accept multiple forms of payment, including cash, credit card, and mobile payments.

Today, mobile payments are mainstream. Consumers and merchants are both accustomed to paying for purchases via a mobile device. Before it was commonplace to use mobile payments, retail stores used cash registers or computer-based systems that worked as cash registers. These are called point-of-sale (POS) systems. Many POS systems will help you set up product and service pricing quite easily. Most allow for discount/coupon codes, special pricing for a limited timeframe, bundled pricing when buying multiple products/services, buy one/get one for free, etc. It is very affordable to use point-of-sale systems built directly for the iPad to keep your business costs low but obtain high value for sales reporting, tax collection, and customer tracking.

Point-of-sales systems used to be expensive, complex systems that required a significant hardware and software investment, as well as extensive training. Today, it's easier than ever to get up and running with a POS system, so simple even the Girl Scouts can use it for door-to-door cookie sales.

Square Up provides several options based on the type of business you have: brick-and-mortar or "on-the-go."

Learn more about Square Up POS solutions at squareup.com.

Think about your options as a business owner to make it as easy as possible for your customers to access and purchase your products. Keep in mind social media networks are extended sales channels for your business. Social commerce in the US grew from $3 billion in 2012 to $14 billion in 2015 and is expected to have exponential growth (Morris, 2018.) It's not only a viable sales channel for companies of every size, but it's on track to become the primary method to buy.

Have you thought about how you can leverage both digital and brick channels for your business?

LET'S PUT IT INTO ACTION

Where should Ophelia sell her chocolates? Establishing her business in the old candy store in the town center has been her dream since the location became available. Ophelia jumped at the chance to get the storefront. She took the lease agreement to her small business lender and discussed financing options to get her business up and running. Ophelia could easily transform the existing commercial kitchen into what she needed in order to craft her own chocolates. A few modifications to existing equipment would be required, but it would be easier and more cost-effective than renting a commercial community kitchen across town. Ophelia and her lender ran the numbers, so she knew what her monthly costs would be for kitchen improvements and to lease the space. Initially, Ophelia will use the store location (brick) as her primary sales outlet, with online sales (click) as secondary. At some point, she will want to increase the volume of chocolates produced and work with a manufacturer. Ophelia will still participate in farmer's markets, arts and crafts fairs, and special events in her community. She worked with her local Department of Revenue to learn about sales tax licenses and special permits to sell her products around her city. Each US state has a Secretary of State website, which provides details for filing sales tax and registering your business. This is a link to a directory for all fifty Secretary of State offices: thebalance.com/secretary-of-state-websites-1201005.

Ophelia also wants to make the most out of virtual sales channels. She has a freelancer friend who works with small businesses to create websites and manage social media strategies. Ophelia decided she would build a digital identity and marketplace in parallel with her brick-and-mortar storefront. She was counting on appealing to broader geographies to bring in revenues and to build a broader customer base. Ophelia could use her family to help fulfill digital orders, and she would look into special packaging to keep the chocolates from breaking and melting when en route to customers. In addition, she wanted customers to experience the essence of her brand as soon as they opened the box. Ophelia realized she needed to step up packaging and figure out the best method to ship. The US Postal Service has boxes in just the right size for her to use, for free. Plus she could preprint shipping labels from her home or office and have the packages ready to go. An extra bonus would be to have the postal worker pick up her packages from her home or office, saving her time driving to and from the post office and waiting in line once she was there. Ophelia thought that the US mail would suffice for her business but she explored other options, including FedEx and UPS. The final decision would be made with her accountant to see which service would bring her the biggest bang for her buck.

The two approaches (brick-and-mortar and digital) go hand-in-hand for Ophelia, as they are equally important to the growth and sustainability of her business.

How to Promote Your Product to Targeted Customers

You have a solid foundation in place for the value you plan to create; you identified the problem it solves and for whom you are solving it; you understand your business model and you created the pricing strategy; and you decided where your customers will buy your product. The final piece will be to inform target customers your business exists. It's time to promote your brand.

Now we will discuss the five elements of promotion, which tells the story about your brand and products. Storytelling is a powerful way to inform and educate. When done right, the message will resonate with the audience you would like to reach. The goal of your promotional efforts is to have customers buy your product and to share their experience of your product with others.

I'm a firm believer in selling without gimmicks. You don't need gimmicks if you built the right value for the right audience and are using the right message at the right time to prompt them to buy. It can and should be that simple.

However, there are some industries that rely only on a numbers game. Efficiency doesn't matter; only numbers matter. They put up invasive banner ads on websites that they believe will deliver a certain number of impressions. Statistics show that a certain percentage of those impressions will actually generate clicks and a certain percentage of those who click will actually buy. If this approach works for your business, more power to you. It is my belief that invasive ads are akin to shouting in the face of your potential customers, relentlessly. It's more of a turn-off than a turn-on. Personally, I stay clear of those types of businesses as a consumer and as a consultant. They have their formulas; they don't need to provide value or build lasting relationships with customers. They are building sales machines and spending a lot of money to convert impressions into sales. I believe this particular customer acquisition approach is not sustainable. It may bring in the short-term cash flow at a high cost, but it typically will not translate into customer loyalty, which is key for a sustainable business.

Let's take a quick look at the myriad of ways you can promote your product and brand to your target customers once you decide to launch your business. It's important to select the elements that make sense for your business. For instance, it may not be appropriate for your company to spend millions of dollars on a Super Bowl ad if you own a small mom-and-pop type of business.

If you're feeling overwhelmed by all the steps needed to promote your brand, don't worry. I created a handy checklist to help you organize what you can apply to your business. It's downloadable from: 20stepspublishing.com/gonogo-templates/

These options are FYI, for you to know what is possible. It

is not a comprehensive list. It's simply to create awareness of what will be coming down the pike after you make a Go decision to proceed with your business idea.

ADVERTISE

Take a smart approach to spending money to promote your product. Look for the potential return on investment (ROI) to determine if it will be worthwhile. Many sales people will tell you it requires spending money to make money because you have to build brand awareness. That's true. However, in today's global marketplace, it's easier than ever to build brand awareness for free or on a shoestring budget, thanks to social media. Spend when and where it makes sense. Be sure your potential target customers will be on the receiving end of your message and have a call to action (CTA), ultimately leading to the purchase of your product. Generating noise with your message to see what will stick is not a strategic approach, and you will be flushing money down the toilet.

There are several types of advertising channels:

Radio: targeted local, regional, or national. It can be very effective, if your target audience listens to specific radio stations. When trying to understand who your target customers are, find out if they listen to the radio, and (if so) what their favorite stations are and what time of day they most listen. This will help you spend much more effectively. If your audience doesn't listen to the radio (they prefer Spotify and other options), then don't spend in this area.

Television (TV): targeted local, regional, or national ads, particularly with the cable operator in your area. There are great deals available when these operators have plenty of inventory. You could have your ad run during TV shows and news broadcasts that may be cost-prohibitive for you. But, because you purchased spots at just the right time at a price that was affordable for your business, you could luck out and have your spot air during prime time when your target audience is watching a specific program.

Print: from magazine and newspaper ads and advertorials (a paid placement) to postcards, flyers, inserts, and more, there are many opportunities for you to get your message to your audience in print form. However, don't just assume your audience reads the local newspaper or top magazine. The more you understand who your customer is, the more targeted you can be in print ad selection.

Outdoor: The sky is the limit for outdoor advertising, sometimes literally! Think of strobe lights with logos embedded (à la Batman's signal), light shows and murals on buildings, billboards (static and digital) on the road and in stadiums, airports, and other venues, bus/car/train wrappers, airplane banners flying over stadiums and events, etc. Whatever method will be most effective for your target customer to see your message is what you should select, if you determine this is an effective method to reach your audience.

Digital Advertising

O Daily deals or local deals: similar to a Groupon or Liv-
ingSocial. These offers are a great way to *acquire* new
customers and to get cash in the door; however, gen-
erally speaking, it's not viable for repeat business and
customer loyalty. Some new customers may fall in love
with your product and continue to buy after their first
experience, but they are the exceptions.

O Banner ads and sponsorships of websites: Spend only
when it makes sense for your target audience and it's
not "in-your-face" or invasive advertising. It's ideally a
niche website, catering to exactly your audience needs.

O Pay-per-click, also known as search engine marketing
(SEM): This approach represents key word buys on
Google, Bing, Yahoo, and other search engines. Your
business will appear in search results, and you only pay
when someone clicks to go to your landing page or
website. If properly managed, this can be a very cost-
effective way to reach customers searching for your
type of product. It can be tedious to manage and to
discover which keywords provide the biggest bang for
your buck. Google AdWords (google.com/adwords)
has many resources to help you figure it all out, such
as video tutorials, webinars, and articles. If you decide
you want to become an expert on Google AdWords,
they also provide certifications and training. If you
don't want to take the time to become an expert in this
area, hire a freelancer to manage it for you.

O Business listings on Google, Yelp, and directory listings that cater to your type of business are typically free for a basic business listing, and you can pay for premium additions to your listing.

Events and Co-Op Advertising

O Sponsorships of events: from small local events (farmer's markets, county fairs, charity, and fundraising events) to global online events (industry conferences, tradeshows, workshops, seminars, classes, etc.). Look for opportunities where your target customer will be participating and where they can see and hear your message.

Partnership and Co-Op Advertising

O This is a great way to split the costs with other companies. Speak with your suppliers: there may be co-marketing or joint marketing opportunities available to you at nominal rates.

Corporate Branding

O Signage/branded materials including marketing swag, which are promotional items with your brand name.

O Storefront signage (inside and outside) or corporate identity materials (such as business cards and packaging for products).

○ T-shirts, baseball caps, or golf shirts.

○ Car wrappers and bus wrappers.

○ Pens, notepads, or water bottles.

Purchase what works and makes sense. Don't waste money on items that won't translate into potential buyers of your product. If you are a doggie day care provider, perhaps having frisbees with your logo and a paw design on it would be appropriate, since many dog owners use frisbees with their dog.

LET'S PUT IT INTO ACTION

Ophelia knows her customers will use all of their senses when they visit her store. She can create just the right atmosphere.

○ **Visually** attractive and enticing from the outside, so customers want to step inside. Lighting, signage, store layout, design, and colors are all important.

○ **Aromas** to make their mouth water once they step inside.

○ **Tantalize the taste buds** when customers try free samples.

○ **Soothing sounds** once they step inside, to cause customers to linger, look, and **touch** products on the shelves available for purchase. The five-sensory experience and the customer service will hopefully provide a favorable customer experience in the store. When customers feel good experiencing what the business has to offer, they'll keep coming back for more and spread the word to others as well.

CONTENT MARKETING

It seems to be the latest buzz in marketing, but it's not new. Content marketing basically means educating your potential customers across many different mediums. Content marketing has been in existence since peddlers were selling their goods hundreds of years ago. In 1732, Benjamin Franklin published his annual *Poor Richard's Almanac* as a way to promote his printing business (Content Marketing Institute, 2018.) Peddlers of goods, such as tobacco and soap, would put flyers up in the town square to promote the products. Advertisements and content marketing have a long history in addressing consumer needs and wants. Today, content marketing is experiencing a rebirth of sorts, with emphasis on educating potential customers rather than blatantly selling to them. By creating a piece of content that has value to your target customer, such as an e-book, white paper, survey report, video, podcast, webinar, etc., and informing them about the latest and greatest happening in the industry or with your product, people will respond. There are a number of ways to utilize content marketing, such as:

○ **Website:** it is a sales channel, as well as a place to inform and educate.

○ **Mobile Apps:** Small businesses can optimize their

website to be mobile-friendly. For example, the website may be responsive and viewable on a smartphone or tablet, but it could be a bit clunky when making a purchase. A mobile app helps streamline the user experience and buying process to make purchasing as simple and intuitive as possible. Domino's was mentioned earlier as one of the leaders in streamlining the purchasing process via websites, mobile devices, and other internet accessible devices (smartwatches, car apps, etc.). Be sure the content can be read on mobile devices very easily.

○ **Social media networks:** word-of-mouth (WOM) marketing and one-to-one (1:1) marketing at their finest. Global reach is in anyone's grasp. Focus on content that is meaningful to your network.

○ **Email campaigns:** Numbers don't lie; even though millennials do not prefer email, it is still a very effective way to send the right message to the right customer at the right time. Thanks to marketing technology tools, you can slice and dice your customer base to send one type of offer to one set of customers and a completely different offer to another set of customers—all with a push of a button. Be sure the subject line and content of the email are relevant to your audience.

○ **Organic Search:** Often referred to as Search Engine Optimization (SEO), it's a way to be found on page 1 of a search results page. Why is page 1 so important? 98% of searchers never go to page 2 and beyond. Instead, they go back and refine their search (Digital

Summit, 2016.) This is called a long-tail search. Adding more descriptors to keywords will provide more precise results. People don't just want results, they want accurate results for what they are looking for. Website technologies help you optimize your site to organically rank higher in search results.

○ **Paid search or pay-per-click:** You can purchase keywords to ensure you show up on page 1 for very specific searches. Google now has paid keyword ads in the center and top of the results page, rather than in the right navigation area, as they had done for years. It's difficult for users to tell if they are paid versus organic search results. Click rates are now higher. Content is key to show up in search results—and the content comes from all digital sources, such as your website and social networks.

○ **White papers, blog posts, workshops, seminars, webcasts, podcasts, and e-books:** if you have something to say, put it in writing and give it away. You can collect data about the person accessing your free content, or not. It's up to you. You can build an email list quickly, as well as ask for other optional information, such as address and mobile phone number, before the content can be downloaded. Be strategic about what you put out there as content. Don't just throw information into the wild blue yonder. Put compelling information out there that will cause your target customer to pause, take notice of your message, and then seek out more information about your brand and product.

Customer Relationship Management (CRM)

○ **Customer marketing:** There are free CRM tools available in the market to help you track your customer data in one view, such as SugarCRM (sugarcrm.com). You no longer have to keep email addresses in one system or list and mailing addresses in another system. This makes it easy to print labels for shipping while maintaining a separate system to look at sales data. You can now have one view into your customer data, segment it, send tailored messages, manage rewards, and thank them for referrals. There are many choices for small business to start with for free, and as your business grows, you can upgrade to get more features and value for small monthly subscription fees. Retention strategies are ideal for preventing customer churn.

○ **Referral programs** are a quick and easy way for you to thank customers for telling their friends about your product or service. There are many turnkey systems available, targeted to small businesses to streamline tracking of referrals and rewards. Gigbee is a leading platform and can be found at gogigbee.com. Referral programs are an important part of a customer acquisition strategy.

○ **Loyalty and reward programs are essential**. As they say, customer satisfaction is fleeting, but loyalty is forever. Your goal is to build a loyal customer base. It's key for sustainability, growth, and profitability. Create a rewards/loyalty program that makes sense for your business as well as your customers. You want to incentivize them with rewards and potentially upsell their purchases, so they buy more. Upselling existing customers is an ideal way to increase the customer value for your business. The tools are out there; you just need to use them. Upserve.com, LevelUp (thelevelup.com), and Punchcard.com are ideal for small businesses.

DIRECT MARKETING

- **US Mail ("snail mail")**: The US Postal Service is happy to see that companies are still sending catalogs and other types of mailers. It's a way to augment outreach. Classics such as L.L Bean and Land's End continue to mail them, which drives digital orders. Call to action (CTA) to place orders from catalogs is still viable. It's ideal for small businesses serving a specific geographic area.

- **Text campaigns**: Customers will opt-in and agree to receive text messages from brands that deliver promotions and savings or special deals for customers. Text campaigns result in instant delivery, and hopefully instant response from your customer. Perhaps you are a restaurant or pub with a drop-in business between two p.m. and four p.m. You can promote special deals for that timeframe to drive increased business.

- **Geofencing or geofilters**: This technology leverages hyper-local advertising to get your customers to engage with your brand. You can provide a compelling offer or incentive for a call to action. Snapchat is just one platform that leverages geographic locations for bringing brands and fans together. Companies such as Locate (getlocate.com) and Simpli.fi cater to companies of all sizes.

SALES PROMOTIONS

Flash Sales: Done in-store, online, and even social platforms, such as Pinterest, Instagram, Facebook, Twitter, and Snapchat, flash sales are very effective ways to convince customers to buy your product. If you have inventory you'd like to get rid of at a discounted price, offer it in a flash sale and watch your followers jump into action.

PERSONAL SELLING

Personal selling, combined with the ability to accept mobile payments using technologies such as Square Up (squareup.com) and PayPal readers (paypal.com) for smartphones, means there's no excuse for not accepting credit cards. It's easier than ever: so much so that Salvation Army Bell Ringers and the Girl Scouts use them to collect money.

PUBLIC RELATIONS AND COMMUNITY RELATIONS

Public relations and community relations is a way to leverage media outlets in your own backyard. You can submit a news tip to local news outlets regarding the grand opening of your business or when you hit significant milestones. In addition, you can work with local nonprofit organizations or schools to help with fundraising by donating your time, money, products, or services to their cause. It's a great way to give back, as well as build awareness of you and your brand in your own community.

LET'S PUT IT INTO ACTION

Ophelia has a lot to consider. She isn't ready to spend money to formally launch her business just yet, but she does want to understand the elements of her marketing strategy, the people she will need to work with to execute the strategy, and what the overall budget will be. She doesn't want to spend more money than is necessary to get her business off the ground. She considers hiring her freelancer friend to take the tactical promotional activities off of her own plate, so they can divide and conquer the go-to-market plan and share responsibilities. Here are the basic elements Ophelia will address early on, prior to making a Go/No-Go decision:

Corporate Identity

She wants to create the right brand personality and tone of voice to match her vision and brand promise for Ophelia's Chocolates.

She works with a graphic designer to create materials. They settle on a color palette and imagery that is visually appealing and sophisticated, and incorporates Mayan influences to convey life and vitality.

Storefront in the Town Center (Brick-and-Mortar)

Once the corporate identity work is completed, she can use the color palette, logo, and overall brand personality to create a storefront experience—inside and outside.

Product Packaging

Packaging of the chocolates (boxes, labels, bar wrappers, etc.): everything that the customer can take home with them will further extend the brand personality and experience. This applies for both in-store and online purchases. Experience of the brand and product is front and center in all of Ophelia's decisions.

Storefront Online (E-Commerce)

The goal will be to drive online purchases, as well as drive visits to the physical store for customers in her area. This will provide an opportunity to meet more customers in person, solicit feedback, and build relationships with locals and visitors from out of town. She is interested in gathering feedback for future product ideas as well.

Mobile-first design approach to the online storefront is a must. The target customers for this product tend to be tech savvy (particularly moms) and prefer to make online purchases via smartphones or tablets. The buying experience must be simple and intuitive. The opportunity to upsell and cross-sell is vitally important.

Also important to foster are calls-to-action (CTAs) for sharing links, following Ophelia's Chocolates on social media, providing reviews of the chocolates, offering customers the ability to earn referral points and rewards, and more. Call-to-action is what drives people's behavior to "do something." The action can be to purchase a product, download an eBook or article, read a recent blog post, share experiences with the brand or product on social media networks, email their friends, and more. Ultimately, every element of marketing your business should have a call-to-action. Ideally, all call-to-action elements are measurable, so you can monitor what is working and what is not working. All behavior and actions from the website and mobile app should be tracked, using analytics and customer information stored in a CRM tool. There needs to be an easy way to scale or increase traffic and sales, so the site will not crash if there's a spike in activity due to promotion or rapid organic growth. Ophelia realizes this cannot be an afterthought to her storefront; it needs to be carefully planned and launched properly from the start.

Order Fulfillment

Logistics for fulfilling digital orders will also need to be handled carefully from the start. It's fine to handle initial orders from the garage or family room. It will be difficult and overwhelming to manage more than a couple of dozen orders per day, even with the help of her kids. Ophelia looks for warehouse and distribution service providers catering to small businesses to handle fulfillment once orders reach a certain point. Once everything is arranged and ready to go, she can quickly pull the trigger to hand over fulfillment to the center and watch her business grow.

Social Media Presence will be vitally important. Ophelia knows her potential customer base is very active on Facebook, Pinterest, Instagram, Twitter, and Snapchat, plus a few others. Managing one or all of the social media platforms will take time each day: time she will not have. As Ophelia works with her graphic designer on her corporate identity and then with her freelancer for building the e-commerce website and mobile app, she approaches another personal connection who specializes in planning and executing social media campaigns for small businesses. It will be key for this person to understand the brand tone of voice in order to convey the right message. This person will listen and respond to followers, keeping engagement two-way, will push educational and informative content about the product, (i.e. health benefits), and will also highlight customer stories.

Ophelia realizes there will be a lot of work ahead, but with the right freelancers assisting her, she could launch her business and build her brand properly from the start, with triggers in place to help her grow as needed. The challenge will be planning and budgeting.

A full-scale marketing plan is required, so Ophelia can take advantage of all resources and tools available to help her grow her small business. Again, she looks to her freelancers for a recommendation for someone who can build and execute a comprehensive plan. Ophelia doesn't have a large budget for marketing, so she carefully invests in the right type of people to get her to where she needs to be. She's hopeful the initial investment upfront in the plan will reap rewards with sales from both her physical and online storefronts. She hopes engaging in social media will ignite word-of-mouth marketing and referrals to slowly increase her business. Ophelia realizes that providing an excellent customer experience at every touch point is key to customer loyalty. The tiny details will matter.

CHAPTER 6

REALITY CHECK YOUR BUSINESS IDEA

First, start by conducting a SWOT analysis of your business idea.

What are the strengths?

Once you complete your research, you will have a solid understanding of the strengths of your business. This is tied to your value proposition, which is your competitive advantage, and other key success factors pertaining to your business. Simply list the elements that put your business in a position of strength. Strengths can include members of the management team and the expertise they bring to your business, the location of your storefronts (brick-and-mortar and digital), a loyal customer base with a high percentage of repeat business, and so on. Is your product easily replicated by others? If not, then it is a strength.

What are the weaknesses?

You should be honest with yourself as you look at the areas you would like to improve about your business. I have yet to work with an organization that did not have any weaknesses. Perhaps the initial competitive advantage is fleeting and easily replicated, which means there is only a small window of time when it is an advantage. If so, note it as a weakness. Perhaps low cash on-hand or limited access to credit is something you need to overcome; these should be listed as weaknesses as well. Identify the areas where you need to improve, your weak links, and come up with ways to overcome the weakness within a reasonable timeframe.

What are the opportunities?

Opportunities are areas that you can potentially turn into future strengths. Perhaps you have an opportunity to be the first at providing your value proposition in your city. Perhaps there's an opportunity to bring investors to help with low cash flow. Potential partnerships are also opportunities to help your business gain traction more quickly. Record all of the opportunities available to you and your business.

What are the threats?

Understanding the potential threats to your business is critical. Once identified, you can then manage the risk and ultimately overcome the threat. A new competitor may enter the market with a better product or service. The economy can be a threat if it causes consumer spending to decline. Better, faster, or cheaper versions of your solution are a threat. There are many areas to consider, and the primary reason to understand them is to create a plan to avoid them, basically mitigating the risk.

Completing this analysis will create a truthful snapshot of today's reality for your business idea. You will then know where you are: Point A.

LET'S PUT IT INTO ACTION

Ophelia's Chocolates SWOT analysis:

Strengths
O Mayan traditions and recipes passed down in the family.

O Potentially a patent-pending formula. (Ophelia realizes she needs legal advice to file a patent or copyright).

O Delicious and decadent taste unlike anything else on the market; it tastes too good to be sugar-free and lactose-free.

O Can be sold for healthy snack pack treats for moms to include in their kid's lunch; they basically provides sweets without the downside.

O In her local community, she has a following of friends and family who love her chocolates and are huge brand advocates for her.

O By working with the Small Business Administration local office, she has created connections that are invaluable to her for getting her business off the ground, including the opportunity to lease the old candy store location.

○ The brick-and-mortar storefront is in a heavily foot-trafficked area in her community; it is attractive to locals and tourists.

○ She obtained a commercial loan to help her with the two-year lease funding and getting equipment for the kitchen.

Weaknesses

○ A saturated market for healthy chocolate; there are lots of boutique chocolate providers.

○ The deep pockets of major candy manufacturers.

○ Limited funding: only for two years.

○ Currently small batch productions, limited opportunity for growth, and scalability for manufacturing, packaging, and distribution.

○ New brand, new-to-the-world product: need to educate market.

○ Lacking personal relationships with suppliers of raw materials: she is not obtaining discounts.

Opportunities

○ The market is demanding healthy and delicious chocolate with no compromise on taste.

○ She can target specialty groups, including the Diabetes Foundation, lactose intolerant foundations, and specialty natural grocer retailers.

O "Buy Local" is promoted by American Express to incentivize customers to buy from local merchants, which is free promotion for her business if she joins the American Express Merchant Network.

O Selling online can help her build the brand throughout the US during year one and potentially add international shipping for year two and beyond.

O Partnership opportunities with brands to help with production, packaging, and distribution to retailers.

O Obtaining shelf space at retailer accounts locally and then nationally (such as Whole Foods, Natural Grocers, etc.)

Threats

O The recipe could be reverse engineered by bigger companies with sophisticated processes and equipment.

O She has a shoestring budget for marketing and getting the business off the ground.

O She needs potential additional funding to scale the business after officially opening its doors.

O Suppliers may not be able to deliver raw materials in large quantities at a discount or in a timely fashion when she requests it.

O Pricing of raw materials could be volatile, depending upon the season.

O Distribution issues could come up with customers

not receiving their online orders.

O Online orders could be damaged and the chocolates might be inedible. Refunds and guarantees
could be costly as she tries to build the company.
Every loss will hit the bottom line.

When Ophelia makes the Go/No-Go decision, she
will need a plan to overcome the weaknesses and to
mitigate risk for the threats, in order for a successful
launch.

Quick Recap

So far we have focused on knowing where you are (Point
A). Now you need to determine what success could look like for
your business. It's time to move on and work on the marketing
program that could get your business to Point B once a Go
decision has been made.

If you're not sure if you are ready to move on or not, jump
to the appendix to review a checklist to ensure you have covered all the bases for your business. The checklist is your guide
for the planning process and to identify areas on which you
need to spend more time. The best way to approach your business is with both eyes open; you need a clear view of your
options in order to achieve success. You need to identify potential areas for failure, so you can mitigate the risks as much as
possible ahead of time.

CHAPTER 7

DEFINE WHAT SUCCESS
MEANS TO YOU

There are two considerations to think about as you decide what success looks like for your business. First, define the goals you would like to achieve. Second, create the plan to go from where you are today (Point A) to where you want to be (Point B).

Business goals are typically associated with a timeline, such as daily, weekly, monthly, quarterly, and annual. The benefit of measuring in time increments is for comparison. You not only want to see an increase in results over time, but you want to see a comparative increase from the previous window of time, such as month to month, or quarter to quarter. This method helps identify patterns. When you don't quite reach sales goals for a particular quarter, you can review the previous quarter. The comparison allows you to look for clues to understand why there was a decrease or change.

In addition to measuring goals by **time**, you will want to measure goals by **certain attributes** that are meaningful for your business. Typically, it can be number of orders, number of products sold, total revenues, number of new customers, or number of repeat customers.

LET'S PUT IT INTO ACTION

For Ophelia's business, she will care about all of the above, including number of units sold by product line. The data will quickly become her guide as to what products are best sellers, what products sell less frequently (so she can produce fewer of them), and even how she could sell more chocolates if she provides "bundles": grouping products together to provide savings to the consumer. This is particularly beneficial to Ophelia because her product is somewhat perishable, and she will need to sell it quickly so she doesn't have a large inventory on hand that may go stale.

The most important area to focus on when defining your goals is to identify what makes sense for your particular business. If you provide services, let's say accounting, you may want to focus on the number of tax returns submitted on behalf of your clients. If you sell salon services (hair, nails, facials, massage, etc.) and products (such as products for hair care, skin care, and nails), you will track at both the service and product levels to understand your customer's buying behavior across your entire business offering. You can look at bundling services together for a discounted rate to increase the total value for an order. Rather than sell just a haircut and blow dry for $50, there is upsell opportunity to sell shampoo, conditioner, and other hair products. You can increase your revenue for one customer from $50 to potentially $100 or more by adding in complementary products.

I recommend you start with simple goals and add new goals over time as you reach initial milestones. You want to quickly adjust your go-to-market plan if you discover there isn't enough traction with sales. A good rule of thumb to forecast monthly sales is to figure 60% of your grand opening day sales and multiply by 30 (days in the month). Success of opening day for retailers is paramount to future success for your business and is the reason why so much time and energy is focused on having a blockbuster grand opening day and event.

LET'S PUT IT INTO ACTION

Ophelia will start with the following goals:

O Number of orders per day.

O Total revenues per day.

O Number of new customers per day.

O Number of repeat customers per day.

The goals could easily be tracked using her point-of-sale system (POS), such as Square Up, which will be managed on an iPad. Each transaction will be stored in the system and associated with a customer phone number or email address.

Since Ophelia will build her customer database from scratch, she will offer an incentive for providing either a phone number or email address. She will provide an incentive to customers who also register on her website to complete a profile. Profile information is helpful for special promotions, such as birthday discounts, store anniversary discounts, and more. Ophelia wants to develop a loyalty program to encourage repeat purchases.

Customer profiles will accomplish several marketing goals.

First, the customer database will start to grow on Day One and will track every customer's purchase.

Second, Ophelia can target special messages and offers to different groups of customers, based on their buying behavior, to incentivize them to buy additional products and to buy more frequently. In addition, she can offer exclusive products for loyal customers that are not available to the general public.

Third, Ophelia will rapidly create loyalty from customers when she provides additional perks for referrals, customer birthdays, repeat purchases, etc.

Fourth, Ophelia can identify who her VIP customers are and provide "surprise and delight" gifts and deals randomly throughout the year, as a way to say thank you for their loyalty.

Ophelia's customers receive tremendous benefit by sharing their email address or phone number with Ophelia in order to receive discounts, earn perks for their loyalty, and for referring others to the business. Customers like to feel special and many would like to see their favorite businesses succeed. They understand by doing their part to help promote the product and brand, they are contributing to the future success of the business.

Ophelia's primary goal is to focus on building customer relationships. She will have **daily goals** for new customers added to the point-of-sale system; she will also track her **overall total number of customers**.

Once Ophelia has customers in her system, she can easily communicate with them via email and social media. The second marketing goal will relate to **customer engagement** via social networks. Ophelia will track conversations, a.k.a. posts, across the social networks her customers are using.

How will Ophelia know which social channels to use? By having her customers include their social network names in their profile. Out of the gate on Day One, Ophelia plans to establish social media accounts for her business.

Ophelia realizes that marketing, and particularly social media, will require time and attention. However, she realizes the enormous benefit of having conversations with her customers wherever they are spending their time socializing. The time and energy put into managing social media can produce much more for the business than simply purchasing a yellow page ad or ads in general. Ads are a one-way message from your business to whomever happens to see it. There is no dialogue with the customer unless they take action: clicking a banner ad, visiting your website, calling your phone number, or walking into your store. It's difficult to predict action from print ads, and the return on the investment is usually quite small.

With digital ads, you pay for leads that click through to your website. Clicks do not always translate into purchases. It will become a balancing act for your business to understand which vehicles work best to reach your target customers. This is why it is so important to do your homework upfront, so that you understand who your target customers are.

O Does your product solve their problem?

O Are they willing to buy it?

O How do your potential customers get their information (from which resources) and from whom do they prefer to receive recommendations?

You should know long before you open your doors for business what the challenges will be to reach your target customers, and what you can do to simplify the process to reach them.

Once you define what success means to you (your business goals reached in the timeline you selected), then it is time to develop the marketing plan to achieve those goals.

I realize the term "marketing plan" may cause anxiety for new business owners because it conjures up the image of spending a lot of money to hire someone to create the plan or trying to figure out how to do it yourself. You could hire a part-time or full-time employee to handle marketing activities for your business or you could hire a freelance consultant or marketing agency to handle it for you. The above options are a positive path forward. However, these options do require a budget: a budget you may not have when your business is just getting started. My hope is that the simple approach I'm providing in this book will provide you with the basics to move forward on your own, regardless of your experience in marketing. I am providing you with a template based on all of the information you previously gathered in Part 1 of this book. The template can be downloaded from 20stepspublishing. com/gonogo-templates/.

Now it's time to organize the information gathered into an actionable plan.

[INSERT Your Company Name Here}
Foundation Action Plan

Why does your company exist?	*Your reason for being*
Problem you want to solve for your customer	*Clearly define the problem your product or service is solving for your target customer.*
Competitive Advantage	*Clearly define what makes your product or service better than other products/services in the marketplace. You're addressing why a customer will select your product or service over others.* Review the competitive advantage statements created. • Ensure what you stated is fact, not smoke and mirrors, meaning more fiction than fact. • Ensure you have an offering that is truly unique. If you realize the competitive advantage isn't real, or truly unique, you may need to revisit Part 1 and determine if you can solve the problem in a different way. It's likely the value isn't as solid as it needs to be.
Target Market	*Clearly define the audience(s) you are targeting.* If you can't describe them, you don't know who they are, and therefore you will not be able to reach them with your message. This likely means you are solving a problem for no one in particular. If you are solving the problem for "anyone" or

MARKETING TEMPLATE

Customer Problem: clearly define the problem your product or service is solving for your target customer.

Competitive Advantage: Clearly define what makes your product or service better than other products/services in the marketplace. You're addressing why a customer will select your product or service over others.

Review the competitive advantage statements you created. Ensure what you stated is fact, not self-deluding smoke and mirrors. Ensure you have an offering that is truly unique. If you realize the competitive advantage isn't real, or truly unique, you may need to revisit Part 1 and determine if you can solve the problem in a different way. It's likely the value isn't as solid as it needs to be.

Target Market: Clearly define the audience(s) you are targeting. If you can't describe them, you don't know who they are, and therefore you will not be able to reach them with your message. This likely means you are solving a problem for no one in particular. If you are solving the problem for anyone or everyone, I recommend circling back to Part 1 and addressing "who" you are trying to solve the problem for. Your target audiences need to be reachable. Hope is not a marketing strategy. You need to know "what" value you are creating and the problem it is solving, "who" has the problem you are solving, and confirm the "who" is willing to buy your product or service. Otherwise, it's a shot in the dark. Is it any wonder that a large portion of small businesses fail within the first year? Those businesses did not have a solid foundation from the start. The business owners did not understand the "what", the "who", and the willingness to buy of the potential audience. If you have not clearly defined the target markets you would like to reach, circle back to Part 1.

Top Competitors: If you get to this section and say, "I don't have any competitors," it's time to go back to Part 1 and do additional market research. It's likely you haven't dug deeply enough to identify similar offerings and substitute products.

Direct Competitors: Identify businesses providing products or services very similar to yours. A customer could choose you or an available competitor. Ideally, the competitive advantage you create and your reason for being will have the customer choose you.

Indirect Competitors: Identify all the other products and services potential customers can turn to. Your product or service has substitutes; identify the obvious ones. For example, when it comes to note-taking, people can use pen and paper, speak into an audio recorder or voice app on their phone, use a stylus pen for their mobile device, use a productivity app on their mobile device, and so on. Substitute products do exist; you just need to think about what they could be.

Differentiation: Define how and why your product/service is unique. If you are unable to articulate how and why your product or service is different from other products/services in the marketplace, how would you expect your customers to be able to do so? Find the sweet spot for you to compete with, and ultimately beat, your competition. If you are falling short on ideas for how your product is different from other products and unclear about how it stacks up against the competition, go back to Part 1 and do some more market research. You need clarity on this before you go to market.

Business Model: Decide how you are going to make money selling your product or service. One pricing strategy for products is based on your total cost of goods (how much it cost you to make the product) plus a profit margin. In the retail space, the margin is typically 100-300%, and then discounted later if the product isn't selling. Another pricing strategy is value-based. Your total cost is relatively low and the value you provide is relatively high. Value-based pricing is determined by what the market will bear.

Services pricing can be based on the actual service itself or hourly fees. For example, a hair salon may charge a flat fee for a haircut and blow dry and another fee for coloring and highlights. Accountants typically charge by the hour or by the tax return, based on what your needs are. It will be important for you to know that your pricing strategy will bring in profit for your business. Be careful to not price yourself out of the market; if the price is too high, no one will buy.

Messaging: Tell your story. If you have access to copywriters and advertising professionals, by all means, leverage their expertise. But if you're like most, who don't even know where to begin with this task, you will need to become a quick learner. Once you have completed the above sections of this plan, you should be able to simplify your messaging so it's readily understood: what you are selling and why it's better than any other product or service. Begin with key message points, then narrow it down to an elevator pitch (fifteen to thirty seconds), and then sum it up in a few words in a tagline.

O Jot down statements about the value you deliver with your product or service.

O Create an elevator pitch (fifteen to thirty seconds).

O Tagline: summarize your value proposition in just a few words.

○ For brick-and-mortar storefronts, you need to plan for the interior and exterior of your business. You need to attract attention, convey your offering, and encourage people to walk in the door. Once inside, the shopping experience should live up to your customers' expectations: what you want the customers to feel and what action you want them to take (purchase now, purchase again in the future, tell others about your products, etc.)

○ For digital storefronts, you need to plan the digital experience you want your customers to have. First time visitors need to learn quickly about your business. The fewer the clicks, the better the chances they'll take action. Action can be making a purchase, signing up for your email newsletter and promotions, sharing your site to a social network, contacting you directly to answer questions about your offering, and downloading information (brochures, case studies, photos, etc.).

Funding: Where can you obtain funding? The obvious places, such as your personal savings, a bank loan, a friends and family loan (referred to as seed money), angel investors (individuals who are willing to invest in you and your business, in the hopes of getting their investment back with a nice profit within a certain timeframe), venture capitalists (VCs) who will invest in your business for a percent equity of your business (this includes *Shark Tank* investors), and crowdfunding via websites such as Kickstarter (kickstarter.com) and Indiegogo (indiegogo. com). You put your product out there and ask individuals to help you raise a certain amount of money and, in return, you will provide them with some value (whether it's the product or some other type of value (such as a limited-edition t-shirt, coffee mug, or bumper sticker) for supporting your business. Sites such as Printfection.com and Cafepress.com.can help you create affordable, quality promotional items.

Risk Analysis: Identify what could go wrong, if anything, with your plan. What activities may not happen? What timelines may be blown? What if the budget has come up short, and you need more funds? List the potential risks and identify what you can do ahead of time to mitigate them or, if the risk actually does happen, what you can do to overcome the risk. I like to think of this as your Plan B, C, and D. If you anticipate what could possibly go wrong, and then have a resolution ready in advance to pull the trigger on, you're well ahead of the game and focused on being proactive versus being reactive to pitfalls that may arise. You want to be in the driver's seat and control your successful future.

Assumptions: This section is as critical as the previous section. There may be a lot of dependencies associated with your business launch. For example: a business loan getting approved, a business partner coming on board, a lease getting approved, suppliers promising you certain resources by a specified date, and more. There's a whole lot of hope riding on the assumptions for all of those moving pieces and parts. Some of the assumptions may be directly tied to the risks you will mitigate. That's fine. But at least you know where the boiling points could be that might blow your launch plan out of the water. This plan is *your* plan, and it's meant to be a living, breathing document that helps you grow a thriving business. Use it to keep risks and assumptions updated on a frequent basis. A marketing plan shouldn't be created and put in a file or on a shelf, never to see the light of day again. It is a living, constantly evolving plan that will guide you as you build your business. It puts you in the driver's seat to proactively control your company's destiny. The plan can alleviate the need for those Hail Mary passes to get you through the tough times. Plus, you will want to celebrate your milestones as you reach them. You wouldn't think about driving across the country from Point A to Point B (and Point C and Point D) without a map or at least Google Maps, right? The same logic applies to your business. Have a destination in mind, so you will know when you have arrived at that destination.

CHAPTER 8

MAKE A GO/NO-GO DECISION

Now that you have completed all of your upstream work to build a foundation for your business, it's time to review all the data you collected and make a decision to move forward with your idea and launch the business: Go or No-Go, go back and refine your idea and value proposition, and then circle back for additional market research.

There are many activities to track during the Go/No-Go process. You will have several projects to work on, and they can be compartmentalized in order to achieve your goals efficiently and cost-effectively. Project management is a must, and there are many tools to assist you to do it properly.

Trello (trello.com) is a great productivity tool to help you organize projects, lists, and activities. If you can't keep your projects organized and track time to completion, you will quickly become overwhelmed and lose sight of the big picture:

moving forward with your Go decision to launch your business or pivot your plan for now, due to a No-Go decision. Revisit, refine, and refocus on the value you would like to deliver, the audience you would like to deliver it to, the willingness of the audience to buy it, and the ability to reach the audience in a timely and effective manner. Run the numbers to ensure you will not get in over your head, causing you financial duress.

Simply start with a project plan. I created a checklist of launch activities for you to start with. The template can be downloaded from: 20stepspublishing.com/gonogo-templates/

Feel free to customize the list, based on the type of business you have.

LET'S PUT IT INTO ACTION

Ophelia's Chocolates has what appears to be a winning product for her target customers: lactose-free and sugar-free chocolates that taste decadent, rather than like something pretending to be chocolate. She is targeting people with special dietary needs; however, she is pleasantly surprised to hear from friends, family, and her community that the chocolates are appealing to anyone looking for a healthy, sweet treat. That is good to know for Ophelia because she can leverage the fans of her chocolates to help spread the word and become influencers for her product. Influencers and brand advocates are fans of the product or service and love to share their discovery within their own community of friends and family. This is word-of-mouth marketing at its finest.

Ophelia would like to officially get her business off the ground in her community by opening a storefront in an area that is heavily foot-trafficked. She discovered from the local chapter of the Small Business Administration (sba.gov) that she has access to commercial lenders and commercial realtors to help her find the right storefront in the heart of her city alongside other small businesses, at an affordable rate.

The ideal location attracts both local customers and visitors to the city. This will help increase brand awareness and allow for more free tastings.

Word-of-mouth marketing is going to be critical for her, since the business is running on a shoestring budget.

Ophelia has identified many goals for herself and the business; however, she wants to be realistic and set herself up for success, so she narrows the list to five goals:

1. Break even within twenty-four months (the length of her commercial loan and storefront lease).
2. Acquire new customers daily (starting with low volume the first month).
   - Increase 10% months two to six.
   - Increase 12% months seven to twelve.
   - Increase 15% months thirteen to eighteen.
   - Increase 17% months nineteen to twenty-four.
3. Repeat customers: build up to 10% by end of Year One; grow to 15% for Year Two.

4. Build relationships with customers to increase their lifetime value; invest in a customer relationship management (CRM) tool.
   - Develop a referral program.
   - Develop a rewards program.
   - Create a presence online (e-commerce site) and on relevant social media platforms.
     - Listen and respond frequently to comments, inquiries, and criticism.
     - Respond with empathy to criticism. The goal is to win them over with kindness, and build and maintain a favorable reputation.
5. Expand product line at the appropriate time.
   - Create and test new recipes and flavors based on input from customers.

Download an example of Ophelia's dashboard spreadsheet at 20stepspublishing.com/gonogo-templates/

Ophelia knows if she can carefully watch her spending and accept that she will not turn a profit for the first two years, she could break even within twenty-four months. Ophelia can track her costs and experiment with pricing strategies for bundled products, and—over time—determine what her ideal profit margin should be. Ophelia is cautiously optimistic and does not want to grow too fast. She would like to enjoy building her business, creating fine chocolates for health-conscious customers and developing relationships with her customer base.

CHAPTER 9

RECAP AND ACTION PLAN

GETTING FROM POINT A TO POINT B

Point A Factors in All of Your Market Research.

Talk to potential customers with the problem you are trying to solve, ask for feedback about the value proposition you plan to create to solve the problem, and ask if they would be willing to pay for it. Build prototypes or samples, and obtain more feedback. Rinse and repeat until you have a minimally viable product to go to market.

Point A is Your Business Reality Today

The SWOT analysis is a great tool to understand what your strengths and opportunities are, as well as weaknesses and threats to overcome.

Point B is Where You Would Like To Go

Think of it in terms of navigating your way from Point A to Point B, so you will know when you have arrived at your destination. Point B represents what success will look like for your business at a specific point in time.

O Perhaps you want to add new customer segments or further refine existing customer segments.

O Perhaps your value proposition needs refinement: Do you still have differentiators against your competitors? Do you understand why sales are declining or, at the very least, not increasing? Do you have repeat customers? What percentage of sales are from existing customers versus new customers? Gather the data to better understand how you can refine your offering.

O Obtain feedback regarding your pricing strategy: Are prices too high for the value provided? Are prices too low, possibly creating low perceptions of the value? Do you need alternative methods of payment (credit card types, mobile payments, etc.)? Is your accounting system nonexistent or subpar, so you don't have access to the data you need to understand customers' buying behavior?

O Monitor Sales Metrics. Determine if it is too difficult for your potential customers to purchase your product or service. Do you need to add more outlets or intermediaries to help distribute to meet your metrics?

Are communications metrics being met? The metrics will help you answer the following:

O Is your communications strategy working?

O Are your potential customers hearing your messages?

O Are you engaging in two-way dialogues?

O Are you tailoring your messages to segments within your customer base?

O Are you using a CRM tool to help you manage your messaging?

O Are you updating your content frequently enough?

O Are you finding opportunities to speak: webcasts, webinars, podcasts, seminars, and conferences?

O Are you relying on a sales strategy that is not working?

O Do you need to spend a lot of money to get leads?

O Are your leads not converting?

Whatever your metrics are, be sure they will allow you to take action to quickly adjust your plan, so you can avoid a domino effect of missing your numbers across the board.

Recap Ophelia's Chocolates: Point A

Who: Define Your Target Audiences

O Those with special dietary needs: lactose intolerant and diabetic people.

O Health-conscious people (initially focus on women and mom segments).

What: Define Your Value Proposition, i.e. the Problem Your Product or Service Solves

- ○ Family recipe based on Mayan traditions for creating delicious chocolate with health benefits.
  - ○ Lactose-free ingredients.
  - ○ Sugar-free ingredients.
- ○ Existing chocolates on the market are bitter or lacking in taste.
- ○ POV: people with health conditions such as lactose intolerance and diabetes have special dietary needs that require lactose-free and sugar-free ingredients because lactose and sugar can be life-threatening to some people.

Why: Product Vision

- ○ For people with special dietary needs who indulge in sweets, Ophelia's Chocolates provide a healthy chocolate bar that is lactose-free and sugar-free. Unlike similar products on the market that have a bland or bitter taste, our chocolate tastes decadent and indulgent without the harmful ingredients.

Where: Availability of Your Product or Service

- ○ Retail storefront.
- ○ Website.
- ○ Social media platforms.

How: potential customers learn about your product or service and what it costs to buy it.

○ Price: $5/bar or $20/5 bars (buy four, get one free)
○ Promotion.
  ○ **Create Brand Identity:** define brand personality and tone of voice to match the business core values and mission.

  ○ **Website:** create an ecommerce storefront, which is search engine friendly, so the business appears in search engine results quickly.

  ○ **Blog:** Ophelia will educate her target audiences about the benefits of chocolate, the special dietary needs her products address, and more.

  ○ **Social Platforms:** Ophelia realizes it is important to listen and respond to her target audiences (not just paying customers) who are discussing special dietary needs regarding lactose intolerance and diabetes.

  ○ **Customer Relationship Management (CRM) Tool:** Ophelia selected a point-of-sale system that also serves as a CRM tool. It allows her to build customer profiles, which track the purchase behavior of each customer. In addition, the system she has selected incorporates a referral program and loyalty rewards program. Email marketing campaigns can be segmented by customer groups that she defines.

  ○ **Support Local Organizations:** Ophelia has decided it is important for her to not only educate the market about the benefits of her products, but to be present in the groups as well. She will partici-pate in youth-oriented programs, health-oriented programs (such as the Diabetes Foundation), school groups, and mom groups in her area.

○ **Networking:** Ophelia knows relationships are key to her business success. She plans to attend local small business association events, as well as women in business events, in order to stay informed about small business opportunities.

○ **Advertising:** Ophelia realizes that she needs to spend some money on advertising to build brand awareness, however, she will do so only after she exhausts the free opportunities available to her. A bootstrap budget can be extended a long way if she's mindful of where she spends her money.

○ **Public Relations:** Ophelia doesn't have relation-ships with any members of the local media, but she knows they want to hear about new businesses, so she plans to submit news tips about her grand opening event.

○ **Direct Marketing:** There are many options for small businesses to obtain the marketing materials required to help spread the word. Creating post-cards, business cards, and flyers and passing them out in her local area, such as coffee shops and schools, will go a long way. There are plenty of cost-effective websites that can produce her materi-als quickly and affordably (such as Vistaprint, Moo, and others).

O **Sales Promotion:** Ophelia plans to do a lot of sales promotion in her store, at local fairs and farmers markets, and wherever she can build partnership connections. Once people taste her product and learn about the health benefits, she hopes word-of-mouth will help her quickly generate sales and increase brand awareness of her business within the audiences she cares about.

RECAP: OPHELIA'S CHOCOLATES: POINT B

1. Break-even within twenty-four months (the length of her commercial loan and storefront lease).
2. Acquire new customers daily (starting with low volume the first month)
   O Increase 10% months two to six.
   O Increase 12% months seven to twelve.
   O Increase 15% months thirteen to eighteen.
   O Increase 17% months nineteen to twenty-four.
3. Repeat customers: build up to 10% by end of Year One; grow to 15% for Year Two.
4. Build relationships with customers to increase their lifetime value and invest in a customer relationship management (CRM) tool.
   O Develop a referral program.
   O Develop a rewards program.
   O Create a presence online (e-commerce site) and on relevant social media platforms.
   O Listen and respond frequently to comments, inquiries, and criticism.

O Respond with empathy to criticism. The goal is to win them over with kindness, and build and maintain a favorable reputation.

5. Expand product line at the appropriate time.
   O Create and test new recipes and flavors, based on input from customers.

OPHELIA'S GO/NO-GO DECISION

Ophelia completed her market research and feels confident she has a winning product at a price point her target audience is willing to pay. She has selected how customers will purchase her chocolates (online and in a retail shop). She completed a SWOT analysis and took a look at the funding options: her total costs to launch, plus the risks and assumptions involved. Ophelia is confident in her conservative approach to break even within two years and has some ideas to rapidly grow her business after two years, once she has recouped her investment.

Ophelia has made a Go decision and is ready to move forward and officially launch her business. She has a clear roadmap for where she is today (Point A) and what success looks like for her business, so she will know when she's arrived (Point B). Now it's time to execute the plan and measure and monitor results. Ophelia also knows she will have to pivot and adapt because consumer preferences and the marketplace are always changing.

Now that you have defined what success means for your business and have your goals set and your marketing plan ready to go, you are ready to make your Go decision and launch your business. Congratulations!

CHAPTER 10

LONG-TERM PROFITABILITY

**How to Get There: Deliver Value That Solves a
Problem to an Audience Willing to Pay for it**

It's important to understand the value proposition your
product or solution provides, to whom the value proposition is
targeted, and to know that audience is willing to pay for it. You
could have a great value proposition and know whom it ideally
is targeted to, and that audience could love it, but if they don't
want to buy it, you don't stand much of a chance of building
a sustainable business.

**Loyalty: Build and Nurture Long-Term
Relationships with Customers and Employees**

You will discover, over time, loyal customers who have a
higher customer lifetime value (CLV). This is the cumulative
amount of money your customer has spent with your business

over time. You want to build relationships with each customer, so they will continue to buy from you, as a trusted brand. Think about your personal purchasing behavior with brands. Do any brands come to mind that you have been with for more than one decade? As a consumer, I can think of my favorite brands since I was a kid, ranging from cereal to toothpaste to potato chips to peanut butter. However, as an adult, other than Amazon.com, I can't readily identify a brand I've consistently purchased from for more than two decades. Amazon works very hard at personalized, one-to-one marketing. Through one-click purchasing, they make it easier than ever to order products on any device. If you think about the Amazon model, are there best practices you can adopt from them to apply to your business to help nurture long-term relationships with your customers?

Glean Insights from Customers to Get Value Back to Improve Products or Services

Customers love to provide feedback and suggestions for enhancements. You do not have to wait for them to submit. Proactively ask customers (and employees!) what could be done to improve the product or service you're offering. You can accomplish this by sending out emails asking for feedback, have a submission form on your website, conduct focus groups, distribute online surveys, conduct net promoter score (NPS) surveys, and benchmark yourself against other companies in your industry and talk to them when you have them on the phone, in a social media channel, or face-to-face. Learn more about NPS scores and their importance from Bain & Company's website: netpromotersystem.com.

If you put out a welcome mat to continuously receive

feedback on how you can provide even more value to your customers, and you provide evidence that you acted on the feedback by adding or changing the product/service offered, you will receive plenty of input from your customer and employee base.

The goal is **loyalty**: from customers and employees.

By now you have the foundational pieces you need for your business idea. You have assured yourself it has value to a specific audience willing to pay for it, defined what success means for your business, launched your business, and measured and tracked results via KPIs. You also understand the importance of relationship management, first with customers and employees and then with partners, suppliers, and other audiences meaningful to your business. People like to do business with people they like. It's simple human nature. Treat your business and your audiences with the respect and caring it needs to grow and to thrive, and you have the formula for building a sustainable and profitable business.

Remember, a strong foundation is key for your long-term success. Once the foundation is in place, you continue to evolve as the market and customer needs evolve. It's a continuous, never-ending journey—enjoy it!

If you would like to share your business experience with me, I would be delighted to hear from you! Feel free to visit 20stepspublishing.com/gonogo-templates/ and submit your story. If I publish your story on my website, you will earn a $50 Amazon gift card. I value each reader's perspective and business story.

I hope you found the process of how to research, define, plan, and evaluate your findings useful. As you look at your business idea, it's best to try to view the future state with as much clarity as possible. I personally know dozens of entrepreneurs who believed passion and hard work would prevail no matter what. What they failed to realize is that it takes a lot of understanding of the market and competitors, as well as understanding of potential customer's preferences and willingness to buy, to have a solid chance at success. When I asked entrepreneurs what they would do if they could start all over again, they had the following lessons learned:

○ Take whatever you think it will cost to launch a business and triple it. Only then will it be in the ballpark of actual costs.

○ Never put yourself or your family in financial jeopardy. Excessive borrowing, mortgaging of the home, and draining retirement savings were major regrets.

○ Don't rob Peter to pay Paul. In other words, don't take all the cash coming in the door and invest it in more hard costs for the business, such as inventory. You may never catch up, particularly if you offer discounts for customers to pay in advance for future products or services. You have fewer dollars coming in the door, and you still have to give up a product or service for a longer period of time.

○ Don't burn bridges, particularly with friends and family. It can be great to have people you are close to at your side to build the business with you. However, be willing to lose those relationships if the business is not successful. Families and friendships have been torn apart due to a lack of transparency about what happened when the business headed south.

O Bankruptcy is a last resort, and not one that should be a Plan B. It hurts your credit for ten years and appears in your background checks when applying for jobs.

O Hire an accountant and have them create a system for tracking expenses and revenues. It will be well worth it, as they will manage estimated tax payments, sales tax payments, etc. You don't want to get into trouble with the IRS. Ignorance is not a defense.

O Seek legal advice, as needed. Don't skimp on contracts, partnerships, and potential patent applications. Hire someone who works with small businesses and has reasonable rates that don't put you heavily into debt. It's not a good thing when the only person making money from your business is your attorney.

O Pay yourself last, but do pay yourself. It's common to put any profits right back into the business so you can grow more quickly. However, to do so is not honoring the value you provide to your own business. Even if it's a nominal fee, it's important to honor your value.

O Separate your personal and business finances. Ensure you have a separate credit card, line of credit, and checking account for your business. Comingling personal and business monies can cause you headaches with your accountant and the IRS down the road.

I wish you success on your journey and with making the ultimate Go/No-Go decision! Remember, you should always pay attention to what is happening in the marketplace. Listen for the signals to see if you need to adjust your product based on what your competition is doing, the feedback your customers provide, and new trends emerging in the marketplace. The more flexible and nimbler you become as a business owner, the more you increase your chances for longevity in business.

APPENDIX

Questionnaire: Preparing for a Go/No-Go Decision For Your Business Idea

1. What is your idea?

2. Why did you come up with this idea? What problem were you trying to solve?

3. Did you talk to others about your idea? Were they likely potential buyers?

   ○ What did they say about your idea? What was good? What was not so good?

   ○ Were they willing to pay for your idea?

   ○ Did you officially ask them if they would buy it, or did they say they would buy it without being asked directly?

4. Did you show a proof of concept (POC) to others? How did they react? How many people did you show the POC to?

5. Did you make changes to your POC and show it to the same people again or to more new people? What was the feedback? Were they still willing to buy?

6. What would it cost you to manufacture your product? Do you have minimum quantities you have to commit to? Or are you dependent on others to make your product by hand? Will volume creation of the product become an issue?

7. Is it cost-effective to turn this into a scalable business? Or is it just a hobby or small business with one-of-a-kind, handmade products?

8. Will you make a profit with your product? How much?

9. What are the words and phrases your potential buyers use to describe your concept?

10. Do you have the ability to get information about these buyers, so you can articulate who your first audience is?

11. Where and how does this particular audience get their information? From social media? Friends?

12. Do you have a database of initial buyers you can begin to communicate with?

13. Do you need staff to help you build or sell this product? How many? Salary?

14. How will you deliver your product to your buyers? Online? Online and stores? Third parties? Stores only?

15. What logistics are involved in fulfilling orders? What is the fulfillment process? What are the total costs? Do you have policies for returns, exchanges, refunds, and warranties? How do you handle credit card payments, sales tax collection, and financial reporting?

16. Where do you get your supplies to make your product? What are the costs?

17. Are there ways to prevent other businesses from offering what you have better, cheaper, faster, etc.?

18. Why should buyers choose your product versus others?

19. How many products do you need to create and deliver/ sell to break even? To make a profit?

20. Do you have customers who will provide testimonials: on paper, social platforms, videos, etc., so your story can be told from their perspective?

21. Have you researched sales tax laws in your area (city, state, and federal) and other regulations that may impact your business? Are you limited to selling in the US? What will it take to sell globally?

22. What is the demand for this product? Is there an opportunity for repeat purchases per customer? Frequency of purchases? Other upsell or cross-sell opportunities?

23. Have you thought about referral programs? Loyalty reward programs?

24. Customer experience and employee experience: what's the plan to keep it positive on both sides?

25. Are product sales scalable? How quickly? To what

extent? How large does inventory need to be to handle sales?

26. Is your product seasonal? Is it something that is purchased as a gift for someone else or oneself?

27. Who are the top competitors: direct and indirect?

28. How is your business positioned vis-à-vis competitors? How can you stand out?

29. How do you know the pricing strategy is right?

30. Are you creating the right message for the right customers and delivering it at the right time, so they will take action and buy your product?

31. What company/brand promise are you delivering? Corporate values? Mission and vision? Corporate objectives?

32. Have you created your corporate identity: corporate brand name, persona, and style?

33. Does your business need a content strategy? Do you need to position your business as experts in your industry? What content can be created to demonstrate your credibility and level of expertise?

34. Are you monitoring industry news? Competitor news?

35. Does your business receive ratings from customers, such as on Yelp, Better Business Bureau (BBB), etc.?

36. Have you completed a SWOT analysis for today? Will you continue to update your business SWOT analysis on a regular basis, such as quarterly, biannually, or annually?

37. Are there ways to drive down costs of running your business?

38. Have you registered to attend, exhibit, or speak at upcoming tradeshows, conferences, and expos?

39. Does your product have unexpected uses or benefits? Are you selling to unexpected groups of buyers?

40. Have you researched media outlets to notify about your business, as well as influential bloggers?

41. Do you have business insurance to handle theft, loss of product, damage to property, and safety incidents of employees and customers?

42. Is there an opportunity to resell other company's products and earn a margin from each product sold?

43. Can fulfillment of product orders continue to grow? What are the plans for selling and fulfilling higher quantities of product yourself versus hiring a fulfillment vendor to handle the warehousing and delivery for your business? Packing and shipping products from your garage or home office has its limitations (due to the sheer square footage of those areas in your home). Can you grow from dozens or hundreds of shipments per day or week to thousands? Maybe, maybe not. Outsourcing to a company that specializes in working with businesses that have outgrown their home-based fulfillment would be the next step, but there are extra costs involved.

GLOSSARY

Banner Ads: A form of online advertising; an ad that is inserted in a website page. There are many types of banner ads available. Learn more from *How Stuff Works*: computer. howstuffworks.com/banner-ad.htm.

Best Practice Approach: a technique or methodology that has proven to reliably lead to a desired result.

Brick-and-Mortar: physical presence of a store or business.

Call to Action (CTA): an instruction to the audience designed to provoke an immediate response. "Call now," "find out more," "buy now," or "join our team."

Click and Brick: (a.k.a. clicks and bricks, click and mortar, bricks, clicks and flips, Womble Store Method (WSM), or WAMBAM) is a jargon term for a business model by which a company integrates both offline (bricks) and online (clicks) presences, sometimes with the third extra flips (physical catalogs).

Content Marketing: a form of marketing focused on creating, publishing, and distributing content for a targeted audience online. Learn more at the Content Marketing Institute: contentmarketinginstitute.com/.

Customer Lifetime Value (CLV): a prediction of the net profit attributed to the entire future relationship with a customer. Learn more at Kissmetrics and calculate CLV: blog.kissmetrics.com/how-to-calculate-lifetime-value/.

Customer Relationship Management (CRM): An approach to managing a company's interaction with current and potential customers. Visit Zoho.com to learn how they help small businesses build and run CRM programs.

Differentiator: The business attribute(s) and/or unique value that clearly separates it from the competition in a particular marketplace. A key differentiator should be unique, measurable, and defendable.

Differentiation and Positioning: Differentiation and positioning are strongly correlated and depend on each other. Positioning, which is the process of arranging for a product to occupy a clear, distinctive, and desirable place relative to competing products in the minds of target customers depends on the differentiation, and vice versa. Because, through the differentiation, which is the process of actually differentiating the product to create superior customer value, we can achieve the desired position in customers' minds. Definition courtesy of Marketing-Insider.eu.

Digital Marketing: digital marketing is the marketing of products or services using digital technologies, mainly on the internet, but also including mobile phones, display advertising, and any other digital medium. Definition courtesy of Wikipedia.

Elevator Pitch: A succinct and persuasive sales pitch, sometimes considered ten to fifteen seconds in length to up to a max of thirty seconds. The idea is to describe your business idea in the length of time it takes to ride an elevator.

Geofencing: The practice of using global positioning (GPS) or radio frequency identification (RFID) to define a geographic boundary. Once this virtual barrier is established, the administrator can set up triggers that send a text message, email alert, or app notification when a mobile device enters (or exits) the specified area. Definition courtesy of Geomarketing.com. (geomarketing.com/geomarketing-101-what-is-geofencing).

Influencer Marketing (or Influence Marketing): A form of marketing in which focus is placed on influential people rather than the target market as a whole. It identifies the individuals who have influence over potential buyers and orients marketing activities around these influencers. Definition courtesy of Wikipedia. Learn more from this *Forbes* article, "Why Influencer Marketing will Explode in 2017": forbes.com/sites/ajagrawal/2016/12/27/why-influencer-marketing-will-explode-in-2017/#6145855620a9.

Key Performance Indicator (KPI): A type of performance measurement. KPIs help you track what's important for your business. Learn more from *Impact Bound*, "10 Marketing KPIs You Should be Tracking": impactbnd.com/the-10-marketing-kpis-you-should-be-tracking.

Leads Groups: networking groups designed to develop and build trusted relationships with other members of the business community, educate other group members regarding your product or service offering, and ultimately share leads to help one another grow your respective businesses.

Long Tail Keywords/Long Tail Search: Three and four keyword phrases which are very, very specific to whatever you are selling. Whenever a customer uses a highly specific search phrase, they tend to be looking for exactly what they are actually going to buy. Definition courtesy of Wordtracker: wordtracker.com/academy/keyword-research/guides/long-tail-keywords.

Loyalty Programs: A rewards program offered by a company to customers who frequently make purchases. A loyalty program may give a customer advanced access to new products, special sales coupons, or free merchandise. The programs are designed to encourage customers to continue to shop at or use the services of businesses. Visit bellycard.com to learn more about small business loyalty programs.

Market Segment: A group of people who share one or more common characteristic, lumped together for marketing purposes. Each market segment is unique, and marketers use various criteria to create a target market for their product or service. Definition courtesy of investopedia.com.

Onboarding: helps new hires adjust to the social and performance aspects of their jobs so they can quickly become productive, contributing members of the organization. Definition courtesy of the Society of Human Resource Management (SHRM): shrm.org

Organic Search: A method for entering keywords into a search engine. Organic search results are listings on search engine results pages that appear because of their relevance to the search terms, as opposed to being an advertisement. Definition courtesy of SearchEngineland.com

Paid Search: Also known as pay-per-click (PPC), a business advertises within the sponsored listings of a search engine or a partner site by paying either each time your ad is clicked (pay-per-click (PPC)) or (less commonly), when your ad is displayed (cost-per-impression (CPM)).

Pain Points or Problems: real or perceived issues experienced by consumers and businesses. Solutions are created to solve pain points or problems by delivering value.

Point of Sale Systems (POS): completes and tracks transactions between a consumer and the merchant at the time of sale or point of sale. Back in the day, merchants simply used cash registers.

Point of View (POV): a meaningful and actionable problem statement that will allow you to brainstorm in a goal-oriented manner. Your POV captures your design vision by defining the *right* challenge to address in the ideation sessions. A POV involves reframing a design challenge into an actionable problem statement. Learn more at the Interaction Design Institute website: interaction-design.org/literature/article/stage-2-in-the-design-thinking-process-define-the-problem-and-interpret-the-results.

Pricing Strategy: One of the four major elements of the marketing mix is price. Pricing is an important strategic issue because it is related to product positioning. Furthermore, pricing affects other marketing mix elements such as product features, channel decisions, and promotion. Learn more at netmba.com/marketing/pricing/

Product Offering: An offering in marketing is the total offer to your customers. An offering is more than the product itself and includes elements that represent additional value to your customers, such as availability, convenient delivery, technical support, or quality of service. Definition courtesy of yourbusiness.azcentral.com

Product Vision: The overarching goal you are aiming for: the reason for creating the product. It provides a continued purpose in an ever-changing world, acts as the product's true north, provides motivation when the going gets tough, and facilitates effective collaboration. Definition courtesy of romanpichler.com

Proof of Concept (POC): a demonstration, the purpose of which is to verify that certain concepts or theories have the potential for real-world application. POC is a prototype that is designed to determine feasibility but does not represent deliverables. Definition courtesy of techopedia.com

Public Relations (PR): public relations is about influencing, engaging, and building a relationship with key stakeholders across a myriad of platforms in order to shape and frame the public perception of an organization. Definition courtesy of the Public Relations Society of America: prsa.org/all-about-pr/

Referral Programs: The practice of building a base of customers or clients by obtaining support from specific sources. It is a way for business owners to get existing customers and friends to promote their business. Learn more at gogigbee.com

Return on Investment (ROI): the result of a calculation that tells you the bottom line return on any investment. The formula is ROI = (Gains: Cost)/Cost. Definition courtesy of investopedia.com

Scalability or Scalable: the capability of a system, network, or process to handle a growing amount of work or its potential to be enlarged to accommodate that growth. Definition courtesy of Wikipedia.com

Search Engine Marketing (SEM): buying traffic through **paid search listings**. Definition courtesy of Searchengineland.com

Search Engine Optimization (SEO): earning traffic through unpaid or free listings. Definition courtesy of Searchengineland.com

Social Networks: An online platform that people use to build social networks or social relations with other people who share similar personal or career interests, activities, backgrounds, or real-life connections. Examples of social networks include Twitter, Pinterest, Snapchat, Instagram, Facebook, LinkedIn, Google+, etc. Definition courtesy of Wikipedia.

Sustainability: Managing the triple bottom line: a process by which companies manage their financial, social, and environmental risks, obligations, and opportunities. These three impacts are sometimes referred to as profits, people, and planet. Definition courtesy of lexicon.ft.com/

Target Audience: a particular group of consumers within the predetermined target market, identified as the targets or recipients for a particular advertisement or message. Definition courtesy of Wikipedia.org

Tribe: A brand tribe is a group of people who are linked by a shared belief around a brand. Its members are not simple consumers, they are also believers and promoters. Definition courtesy of Wikipedia.org

Unique Selling Proposition (USP): differentiates a product from its competitors, such as the lowest cost, the highest quality, or the first-ever product of its kind. A USP could be thought of as "what you have that competitors don't." Definition courtesy of Whatis.Techtarget.com

Value Proposition: an innovation, service, or feature intended to make a company or product attractive to customers.

Word-of-Mouth (WOM): customers influenced by consumers recommending a product or service to their connections (friends, family, colleagues, etc.)—a major element within social networking. Learn more at the Word Of Mouth Marketing Association: womma.org/

Resources and Endnotes

ABC

"Watch Shark Tank TV Show - ABC.com." ABC. Accessed August 20, 2018. abc.go.com/shows/shark-tank.

CDC

Centers for Disease Control and Prevention. Accessed August 20, 2018. cdc.gov/features/diabetesfactsheet/.

Content Marketing Institute

Endnote 12 – "A Brief History of Content Marketing [Infographic]. Content Marketing Institute. Accessed August 19, 2018. contentmarketinginstitute.com/wp-content/uploads/2016/06/History-of-Content-Marketing-Infographic-2016-1.pdf.

Digital Summit

"Digital Marketing Conference | July, 2016 | Digital Summit Denver." Denver. Accessed August 21, 2018. denver.digitalsummit.com/.

Facebook

"Company Info." n.d. Facebook Newsroom. Accessed August 19, 2018. newsroom.fb.com/company-info/. (Facebook, 2018.)

Gottfried

Gottfried, Miriam. "No Growth, No Profits for Twitter." The Wall Street Journal. Last modified February 9, 2017. wsj.com/articles/no-growth-no-profits-for-twitter-1486666296.

Kickstarter

Accessed August 20, 2018. kickstarter.com/projects/1250439912/popsockets-iphone-case-it-pops-props-kicks-and-cli/comments.

Mind the Product

"Inspiring Teams with Product Vision." Mind the Product, Last modified June 7, 2017. mindtheproduct.com/2017/01/inspiring-teams-product-vision/.

Morris

US Social Commerce stats: Morris, Susannah. "Where Social Commerce Revenue Comes From [Infographic]." HubSpot Blog. Accessed August 19, 2018. blog.hubspot.com/marketing/social-ecommerce-revenue-infographic.

Statista

"Twitter MAU Worldwide 2018 | Statistic." n.d. Statista. Accessed August 19, 2018. statista.com/statistics/282087/number-of-monthly-active-twitter-users/.

The Physicians Committee

Anonymous. "What Is Lactose Intolerance?" The Physicians Committee, Last modified August 15, 2011. pcrm. org/health/diets/vegdiets/what-is-lactose-intolerance.

Unicornomy

Economy, Unicorn. "How Does Twitter Make Money and Twitter Business Model." Unicornomy, Last modified March 26, 2017. unicornomy.com/how-does-twitter-make-money/.

Handy List of Website URLs

○ PopSockets: PopSockets.com

○ Secretary of State: 50 States Directory: thebalance.com/secretary-of-state-websites-1201005

○ Google Alerts: Google.com/alerts

○ Google News: News.google.com

○ Google Adwords: google.com/adwords

○ Google Business Listing: google.com/mybusiness

○ Flipboard: Flipboard.com

○ SharkTank: abc.go.com/shows/shark-tank

○ Point of View: downloadable PDF for defining the process: dschool-old.stanford.edu/sandbox/groups/designresources/wiki/36873/attachments/74b3d/ModeGuideBOOTCAMP2010L.pdf

- ○ Yelp Business Listing: biz.yelp.com/
- ○ SugarCRM: sugarcrm.com
- ○ Square Up Space Website Builder: squarespace.com
- ○ Square Up: squareup.com
- ○ PayPal: paypal.com
- ○ American Express Shop Small: americanexpress.com/ us/small-business/shop-small/
- ○ Upserve: upserve.com
- ○ Trello: trello.com
- ○ Gogigbee: gogigbee.com
- ○ Wix Website Builder–wix.com
- ○ Weebly Website Builder–Weebly.com
- ○ Nextdoor Business Directory: nextdoor.com/business
- ○ Angie's List of Contractors: angieslist.com
- ○ Home Advisors list of Contractors: homeadvisors.com
- ○ Better Business Bureau: bbb.org
- ○ US Chamber of Commerce: uschamber.com/
- ○ Facebook social network: facebook.com
- ○ Twitter social network: twitter.com
- ○ LinkedIn social network: linkedin.com
- ○ Instagram social network: instagram.com
- ○ Pinterest social network: pinterest.com
- ○ Snapchat social network: snapchat.com
- ○ LevelUp Rewards service: TheLevelUp.com.

○ Punchcard Rewards service: punchcard.com/

○ Locate Geofencing solutions: getlocate.com

○ Simpli.fi geofencing solutions: simpli.fi

○ Kickstarter Fundraising site: kickstarter.com

○ Indiegogo Fundraising site: indiegogo.com

○ GoFundMe site: gofundme.com

○ Printfection promotional items: printfection.com

○ CafePress promotional items: cafepress.com

○ Small Business Administration: sba.gov

○ Net Promoter Score: netpromotersystem.com/

DOWNLOADABLE TEMPLATES

From 20stepspublishing.com/gonogo-templates/

O **Checklist**: the handy marketing checklist to ensure you cover all aspects addressed in this book.

O **Startup Action Plan Template**: an action plan template for your startup business.

O **Launch Ideas Template:** launch ideas to consider if you are opening a physical store.

O **Ophelia Dashboard Spreadsheet:** a sample spreadsheet template for Ophelia's metrics to monitor.

SHARE YOUR BUSINESS STORY WITH US!

If you would like to share your business experience with me, I would be delighted to hear from you! Visit 20stepspublishing.com/gonogo-templates/ and submit your story. If I publish your story on my website, you will earn a $50 Amazon gift card. I value each reader's perspective and business story.

About the Author

Lauri Harrison is a marketing lecturer at Columbia University, School of Professional Studies. In 2011, she created a graduate level Introduction to Marketing and Marketing Management course and continues to teach it today. Lauri also works for Google, guiding external customers on digital transformation journeys.

Ms. Harrison has a passion for teaching and learning and strives to instill the foundational marketing principles within every student and client she encounters. Ms. Harrison is frequently interviewed by media outlets (CNBC, Eatery.com, *The New York Times Upfront*, and others) for her perspective on trending topics in marketing.

Ms. Harrison earned a master of science degree in marketing from the University of Colorado and a bachelor of business administration degree in marketing from the University of Hawaii. She also completed post-graduate studies at Stanford University as a member of the inaugural graduating class of 2014 for the Innovation and Entrepreneurship (I&E) professional certificate program.

Ms. Harrison has worked with start-up companies since 1995, beginning with her first "dot com": MapQuest. Prior to joining the faculty at Columbia University, Ms. Harrison guest lectured for more than a decade at the University of Colorado (Denver), Colorado State University, Metro State University, University of Northern Colorado, and Denver University. In addition, she has been a panel speaker at industry conferences, including the Women's Vision Foundation, Women in Technology, and Yellow Pages Publishing Association (YPPA).